Seven Sins That Sink Your Family...

and How to Overcome Them

David Raúl Lema Jr., PhD

Maven House Publishing

Seven Sins That Sink Your Family © Copyright 2024
David Raúl Lema Jr., PhD
All rights reserved.

Neither this book nor any part may be reproduced or transmitted in any form or by any means, electronic or mechanical, including photocopying, microfilming, and recording, or by any information storage and retrieval system, without permission in writing from the author.

Unless otherwise noted, all scripture is taken from the *Holy Bible*, New Living Translation, copyright © 1996, 2004, 2015 by Tyndale House Foundation. Used by permission of Tyndale House Publishers, Inc., Carol Stream, Illinois 60188. All rights reserved.

Scriptures marked CSB are taken from the Christian Standard Bible. Copyright © 2017 by Holman Bible Publishers. Used by permission. Christian Standard Bible®, and CSB® are federally registered trademarks of Holman Bible Publishers, all rights reserved.

Scriptures marked NIV are taken from the Holy Bible, New International Version®, NIV® Copyright ©1973, 1978, 1984, 2011 by Biblica, Inc.® Used by permission. All rights reserved worldwide.

Scriptures marked KJV are taken from the King James Version of the Holy Bible. Public domain.

Scriptures marked NET are taken from the NET Bible® copyright ©1996-2017 by Biblical Studies Press, L.L.C. http://netbible.com All rights reserved.

To Jesus Christ,
our Lord and Savior,
who provided the vision to begin and strength to finish.

To JC!
Lord and King forever!

Acknowledgments

I honor and recognize you, the reader, for giving up your precious time to read the insights in *Seven Sins*. Thank you for investing in this book for the benefit of your family and yourself. My prayer for you is that the words of this book can minister to you and your family. May God bless you.

I would also like to thank my beautiful wife of thirty-five years, Milvian. She has put up with me and my nonsense and has done her part so our family ship does not sink. She is one of the reasons why you have this book in your hand now.

This book would not exist without my parents, David and Esther. They not only gave me life but taught me how to live.

Another person who has been a force in making this book a reality is my mother-in-law, Noemi. We lovingly call her Mimi. She believed in me. Thank you, Mimi, for your support. Thank you, also, to my father-in-law, Cesar.

And to my three kids, David, Christine, and Mark, who have sailed on this family ship through thick and thin. Thank you. May your ships sail on smoothly and effortlessly.

CONTENTS

INTRODUCTION	I
1. SINS OF THE FATHERS	1
2. PROUD PARENTS	8
3. ANGRY BIRDS	14
4. LIVING ON THE LAZY RIVER	26
5. LUSTY EYES	38
6. FATTER AND FATTER	49
7. THE WORLD IS NOT ENOUGH	58
8. THE NEIGHBOR'S GRASS	66
9. ESCAPING CAPITAL PUNISHMENT	73
ABOUT THE AUTHOR	81
MORE ABOUT MAVEN HOUSE PUBLISHING	82
APPENDIX A	85
ENDNOTES	87

INTRODUCTION

I really like boating. It doesn't matter whether I'm on a small sailboat or fishing skiff or cruising on a super-large transatlantic cruise ship. The experience is the same—exhilarating! However, anyone who has done any serious boating knows there is always the danger that the ship will sink. No matter what the weather is, the reality is that in the deep caverns of your mind, you know that danger is always tied to boating.

Any boat or ship you're on can sink in many ways—weather factors, extenuating circumstances, the condition or state of the ship, and many other reasons. Nevertheless, one of the quickest ways your ship, regardless of its size, will sink is if your ship is torpedoed by someone or something. Torpedoes are designed to cause massive and immediate damage and can easily sink a ship. A hole in your ship will easily send it down to Davy Jones's locker.

Your family is living on the boat of life. On a beautiful day there is nothing like taking your family for a ride on a boat. Yet there are always dangers looming. You do not want the boat your family is in to sink. In fact, this reality is unthinkable. If your family sinks, you are in deep trouble. Nothing like torpedoes to sink the boat your family is on. You begin to worry day and night about which torpedoes could possibly destroy the boat your family lives on.

Almost everyone I know is worried about their family. I know. I have been there. I have always wondered what it would be like to have a family . . . and lose it. To see the boat your family is on sink. It seems impossible but it is true—one can lose a family in this world. This book is about never having to lose a family that way.

We should not have to think about this right now. But the reality is, we must watch and learn. We should be able to think about this later, but we must think about it now. If we are to overcome the worries about our family's ship, we need to learn how to avoid what can make it sink.

Everyone has fears. Fears for their family. Fears that their family might sink. Fears their family might sink in a deepening abyss of darkness and never see the light of the sun again. The fear of children succumbing to chronic drug addiction. The fear of having a health challenge paralyze your spouse. The fear of losing your job. These fears can keep us from becoming who we really need to be, and keep our family from thriving. We need to take control of this situation before it gets out of control. We need to be rescued!

We will take this fear and turn it around so it can lead to good instead. We will take this fear and realize its possibility of worthiness in God's hand. We will take this fear, overcome it, and make it into a grandstand for faith in God's plan. We will take this fear and make it into the fiber of everything we have been doing so that we come out stronger.

Welcome to overcoming fear! Welcome to this life in your ship. Welcome to a journey that won't sink your ship. Welcome to this discussion and this time together. Welcome to where we want to start.

We start by recognizing the situation you are in. That your family could use some help. Your family is sinking. You may not realize it, but torpedoes have damaged the hull of your family boat. We start by letting you know you are in the right place. In these chapters you'll find the tools needed to begin to take control of your family life. So what are you waiting for? Let's go!

INTRODUCTION

REFLECTION QUESTIONS

After each chapter you will find questions for you to think about key themes from the chapter. After you think about your answers, share your thoughts with someone you feel needs to discuss this topic.

Let's start with some easy questions for practice:

1. Are you worried about your family? If yes, what worries you? Is it a particular family member? If you answered no, why do you think you have no worries?

2. What are your fears for your family? Is your family about to sink? Do you have time to fix the boards but eventually your boat will sink?

PRAYER

After each chapter you will find a specific prayer you can pray dealing with the topic of the chapter. You can make this prayer your own, or use it as it is. These prayers are offered for you to use if you need and want to use them. Let's start with a prayer of thanksgiving.

My dear Father in heaven,
Thank you for giving me the privilege to read this book and apply it to my life. Thank you for giving me this book at this intersection of life and family. Thank you for worrying about my family and giving me this opportunity to think, reflect, and pray for my family. Thank you for loving me and my family more than we deserve. Thank you for wanting to stop the sinking of my family in this ocean we call life. Thank you for knowing the particulars in my life like no other. Thank you for being there to rescue us.
In Jesus's name we thank you. Amen.

CHAPTER ONE

SINS OF THE FATHERS

Since the beginning of time these "sins," as they have been called forever, have been hampering the success of families. In particular, these seven transgressions have been on autopilot since the beginning of time. They have been waiting for you. They are like torpedoes aimed right at your family. This is not a situation of *if* something is going to happen but *when*. These seven sins, while not initially present in the beginning of creation, became a curse for you and your family the minute Eve tasted the forbidden fruit in Eden. At that very moment, these seven things, or sins, made their grand entrance into the tapestry of history and have plagued mankind ever since.

These seven negative behaviors, or as the Bible calls them, sins, have mercilessly destroyed families since the beginning of time. They are like cancers in our families today. These sins are the culprits behind family physical abuse, sexual abuse, mental abuse, divorce, teen suicide, teen pregnancy, social deviancy, mental illness, all types of addictions, poverty, and even murder and many, many other offenses. To take control of your family right now, you must take control of these choices. But how?

The Bible calls these seven sinful behaviors out by name—pride, anger, sloth, lust, gluttony, greed, and envy. They are sins because they function as "in-betweeners." They come in between you and your family and God. Ever since the moment after the fall of creation, these sins have been tormenting humanity. Their only purpose is to drag you and your family deeper into the abyss of sin. And yes, they are quite effective at dragging you into darkness.

You may think your family is safe from harm from these sins. You may even think that since you sometimes go to church, God will protect you from these sins. Perhaps you believe you and your family are the exception to the rule and that these curses will never touch you. Like they say: what you do not know, cannot hurt you. Well, unfortunately, you are too late. These offenses run free and smug in our society. In fact, in our current upside-down culture, people worship these sins as virtues, or worse, consider them as personal rights. Many ignore the curse and accept these sins as simply part of the human nature that defines us and our families. This vicious lie is driving our families straight into the domain of hell. But not hell when you die, hell right here on earth! If any of these seven gain a hold in your family, life will be a living hell. I can cite you first and last name of hundreds of people I have known in my ministry who serve as living proof of this tragedy.

Sadly, all these sins share the same cross-generational effects across time. This is one of the reasons why early in Christian history, the theologians of the church labeled these sins as cardinal, or extremely dangerous, or extremely important. In fact, they called them capital sins. Their penalty was always death in some fashion or another.

This is the sad reality of cross-generational sin. They became known as the sins of the fathers, as they were passed down within families. Perhaps a better descriptor would be the sins of the *parents*. This type of sin is started by individuals in one generation but its effects last well into many future generations of those same families. The children end up paying consequences for sins they did not commit.

The perfect example from the Bible are Adam and Eve. (See

their story in Genesis 1–2.) They were the perpetrators of the original sin in the garden of Eden. They ate the fruit of the forbidden tree, and all humanity has been paying the consequences since. We are the current examples. As parents and grandparents, our sins, if unchecked, will detrimentally affect our children, and their children, and their children's children.

The biblical passage 2 Samuel 21:1–14 brings us a story that demonstrates the problem with cross-generational sins and how to overcome them. It is an anecdote on setting up a barrier to root out the sins and throw them away. This way of getting rid of sins is effective and clear.

The sins of the fathers cannot be ignored. They are a cross-generational reality. The story in the Bible does not have any backdrop or context. It stands independently in the text. The main subjects in this story are practically unknown to us: the Gibeonites. Historians and theologians agree that the Gibeonites lived in their cities in the Promised Land that was allotted to the tribe of Benjamin at the time of the conquest of the land in the time of Joshua.

The Gibeonites were the ingenious people that tricked Joshua and the people of Israel into believing they were from a land far away when, in reality, they were next door neighbors! (See Joshua 9.) Joshua and the people of Israel did not consult with God about this seemingly unimportant matter and instead disobeyed God in making a treaty with the Gibeonites. As a result, the Gibeonites were safe from conquest but became the servants of the Israelites forever. They later served in the temple and provided wood and water for the activities there while the temple still stood.

King Saul, years later and for unknown reason, decided to exterminate the Gibeonites once and for all to solve the Gibeonite nonsense.

He would violate the ancient treaty in the name of national security and unity. The Bible does not tell us, but at some point in time, Saul carried out a great massacre against the Gibeonites to clean out the territory of Benjamin. This act of genocide went against a four-hundred-year-old treaty. Saul decided to ignore the terms of the agreement, but God did not. Neither did the Gibeonites.

So God sent a great famine (See 2 Samuel 21.) Saul was already dead, having been killed in battle with the Philistines. However, a dark shadow loomed behind Saul's life that reached well beyond his years. His genocidal sin mysteriously crossed generational lines and impacted all of Israel. The sin was manifested in a terrible way. Saul desecrated the oath and took the Gibeonites all the way out to the limits of existence, even murdering many of them. This sin would have a huge and lasting effect upon the Gibeonites, and upon the people of Israel.

The consequences of the sins of the fathers are terrible. Saul did what he did knowing it was wrong. Saul was a failure as a king. He died in disobedience to God, having never repented of this and many other sins. The consequences for his family were terrible: his children and grandchildren paid with their lives. His people and country also paid with a high price. Yet Saul never repented. We realize our sin and never repent. Why not?

The scene of a mother keeping a six-month vigil, so the cadavers of her sons were not desecrated by birds and animals is a burning image of deep pain and loss. Rizpah, the daughter of Aiah, is a warning to all of us of the deep pain caused by this generational sin. She watched over the bodies of her two sons—Saul's sons—after the Gibeonites demanded their deaths for what Saul had done to break the covenant with their people and kill many of them.

SINS OF THE FATHER

These scenes must bring out in our lives the threats to us. Birds cunningly swooping over the carcasses of bodies that were sacrificed for an ancient sin. The bitter tears of a mourning mother. The thousands of years it would take for those tears to dry!

Jails today are filled with men and women serving time for their crimes, yet many of them are merely reflections of the sins of their fathers and mothers. The absentee father, the drug-addicted mother, divorced and broken families are common themes in the population of our jails today. We are all more than aware of cocaine babies and children who grow up mentally and physically handicapped because a parent was irresponsible. Parents who were abusive will have abusive children. Hurt people, hurt people.

But what about your family? This certainly cannot apply to you, right? Or are you in this lot without knowing it? What sins did your parents, or grandparents, hand down to you that now are devastating your life, and you may not even realize it? Are you experiencing the guilt of paying for sins that were not even yours to commit? What about the sins affecting your society? Are you a victim of cross-generational sin?

What about your children? Are they victims too? What sins have you committed that impact your family today? What sins will haunt your grandchildren because of you? The consequences of the sins of the fathers/parents are terrible.

Thankfully, there is a solution to this cross-generational sin. The solution is quick but will always bring fear into your eyes. The fix is to make amends, or as the theologians say, to atone for the sins of the fathers as soon as possible.

In the story of Saul and the Gibeonites, David was not going to deter, to allow the cross-generational sin of Saul to cause further destruction to the people of Israel. David knew that something had to be done. Someone had to atone for the sins of the fathers. God demanded justice. Justice demanded retribution.

The demand for atonement must be met. This was one tough situation to deal with completely and with finality. How could one person deal with this problem and bring the peace that comes with forgiveness? As a solution to this evil, David gave the Gibeonites the surviving sons of Saul, and they were impaled before Saul's hometown of Gibeah. Wow. What a drastic solution! It seems inhuman to impale people today. The solution seems to be barbaric at best and over the top at worst. This deed is far away from our reality today.

Yet the board is not erased when you are gone. Atonement is still the solution. So who do we have to impale on a tree from your family? This answer is beyond the realm of the possible for us. Incredibly enough, God took care of this issue for us. To save our families, God took two sticks and some nails and impaled—or better yet crucified—his son on them so that the sins of your family could be atoned. Yes, just like the sins of the fathers can go on for generations and generations, so also the forgiveness of God, through Jesus the Messiah, goes on for generations and generations. You get to make amends! Now. Right now. You can stop the cycle of sin in your family.

Note: Go to appendix A if you need to know the process of how you can stop the cycle of sin in your family right now.

REFLECTION QUESTIONS

1. What do you think about the seven capital sins? Do you believe any of them are about to torpedo your family's ship? Do you see pride, envy, lust, greed, gluttony, sloth, or anger affecting your family today?

2. What do you think about the reality of cross-generational sins? Do you believe you are a victim of cross-generational sin? How has this impacted your family?

3. How does the biblical story of Saul and the Gibeonites resound in your family?

4. Do you think you are guilty of committing a cross-generational sin? How will you make atonement?

PRAYER

My dear Father in heaven,
Please forgive me for carrying the burden of guilt for the sins of my fathers. Please let me atone for their mistakes. Give me the clarity to see their sins and to make atonement for them. Please stop this vicious cycle of cross-generational sin. Please cleanse my family from this curse. Thank you for atoning for this sin through the death and sacrifice of Jesus Christ, your son.
In Jesus's name I pray this today. Amen.

CHAPTER TWO

PROUD PARENTS

I remember when our first child was born. We had been preparing for eight months after the announcement. I painted the child's room pink in anticipation of the daughter the sonogram foretold. I also remember having to paint the room over again in blue when the prognostication changed!

When my child was born, I was so proud to be his father. I wondered, as I held that frail creature in my arms, what kind of legacy I would leave him. I had only good thoughts at the time. I did not realize that much of what we may pass down can be very negative indeed.

Unfortunately, one of the legacies we leave our children is our sin. The first, and most prominent, sin in this list of seven capital sins is pride. A capital sin is considered quite harmful in our lives because it deprives us of life. Pride is the oldest sin and probably the first sin of all. This was the sin that sent Lucifer packing from heaven. It was also the sin that sent Adam and Eve packing from Eden. It is also the sin that sends us packing in our lives . . . to a living hell.

"In Judaism, pride is called the root of all evil."[1] In fact, the very word has an *I* in the middle. Pride refers to having everything swinging around that I. Pride is a selfish sin. Pride only thinks about itself.

The ancient Greeks introduced to us the concept of *hubris*, which was the pride of humans who sought, by whatever means, to stand out. *Hubris* has been defined as arrogance. The Greek gods made sure to punish anyone who had hubris. Incredibly enough, today pride is defined as a virtue as well. In fact, one great leadership guru, John Maxwell, discusses the possibility of two kinds of pride. A common differentiation is made between "authentic" pride (positive virtue) versus "hubristic" pride (negative vice).[2] Now why did Maxwell feel led to make this distinction? Well, many people talk about how proud they are of their work, their service, their lives, their kids, etc. "With a positive connotation, pride refers to a content sense of attachment toward one's own or another's choices and actions, or toward a whole group of people, and is a product of praise, independent self-reflection, and a fulfilled feeling of belonging."[3] We hear talk of gay pride, military pride, family pride, ethnic pride, and so many other prides that the word's meaning dissolves in abstraction.

By definition, "pride is an emotional response or attitude to something with an intimate connection to oneself, due to its perceived value."[4] The Oxford dictionary defines pride as "the quality of having an excessively high opinion of oneself or one's own importance. Pride is inordinate self-esteem."[5] Dictionary.com defines pride as "a high or inordinate opinion of one's own dignity, importance, merit, or superiority, whether as cherished in the mind or as displayed in bearing, conduct, etc."[6] Pride is simply making yourself number one, numero uno . . . and living with the consequences.

The biblical, and spiritual, reality is that God hates pride. The Bible states in Proverbs: "Pride leads to disgrace, but with humility comes wisdom" (11:2); "The Lord detests the proud; they will surely be punished" (16:5); and "Pride goes before destruction, and haughtiness before a fall" (16:18). When pride steps in, God walks out!

It seems strange that we should choose to start with the capital sin of pride. But the truth is that pride is all around us. This pride shows itself in all relationships, even in those we hold sacred.

The reality is that pride can be seen quite clearly in the relationship and role of motherhood. A mother's pride is one specific example of a general spiritual reality. There are many other examples. Yet if not properly understood, confessed, and stopped, pride, even a mother's pride, can deep-sink a family.

Two biblical examples, one negative and one positive, illustrate how two different moms dealt with pride. Salome was a mother whose pride became a problem. She was a faithful disciple of Jesus. She was at the crucifixion of Jesus and also at the empty tomb. (See Matthew 27:56 and Mark 16:1.) She was the wife of Zebedee and the mother of the apostles James and John.

Salome is the mother prominent in Matthew 20:20–28. Her mother's pride prompted her to abuse her closeness to Jesus and make a special request, a proud request, on behalf of her two sons. She saw nothing wrong with her request. So what if other people saw it as trying to get ahead. Of course, Jesus said no. He gently rebuked Salome and her motherly pride. And then Jesus proceeded to give one of the best teachings on radical discipleship and how humility works among his disciples and followers.

Salome's pride went too far. Guiding your adult children to take a prideful stand is not natural. She overbid her stance with her children and Jesus. She definitely went too far for Jesus. Her pride was not a good example, even though she fell for a lie. The lie was the belief in the reward of prominence. She was making a judgment call. And her judgment was called!

The second example is when a mother's humility went way beyond her and impacted her family. This humble mom was none other than Jochebed, the mother of Moses, Aaron, and Miriam (the spiritual leaders of Israel) and the wife of Amran the Levite. (See Exodus 2:1ff.) Note that in the Torah the name of this woman is not even given in the story of Moses and the bulrushes. Her name only appears twice in the Torah and nowhere else in the Bible. (See Exodus 6:20 and Numbers 26:59.) But she was special.

The story tells how she saved Moses from being killed by the soldiers of the Egyptian Pharaoh. (See Exodus 2:1–10.) In a strange twist, "the deliverer of Israel was delivered"[7] by his mom. She gave up her precious son in faith and put him in a basket in the Nile. She cared for him for no more than three short years, then gave him up to be a prince of Egypt, not knowing what would happen to him. She humbly trusted God for her son's future and promptly exited this life. We never hear of her again. This amazing woman, Jochebed, was a mother whose humility became a pattern.

What kind of an influence did this woman have that her three children were the three leading religious leaders of a multitude of millions on a trek to the Promised Land of Israel? Her son Moses, the liberator, was described in the Bible as the meekest man on Earth (See Numbers 12:3.) Her son Aaron was the first high priest of Israel, and Miriam was known as a prophetess. These three were heavyweights in their society. What mother would not want to give birth to three children such as these? Jochebed was a mom that was thinking beyond herself and her needs. Her example of humility began a pattern in her family that lasted beyond her lifetime. Even the children of her children, and their children, and their children's children were impacted by her humility. They were launched into the future with humility as a hallmark, coming from their mom.

So we have seen a negative example of motherly pride and a positive example of motherly humility. Where do we stand today? We stand with the principle that a mother's character reflects in her children. As Rick Warren puts it: "This is true humility: not thinking less of ourselves but thinking of ourselves *less*."[8] This attitude was certainly true of Jochebed and certainly needed with Salome's petition for her sons.

Pride is a sin. Like all sin it needs to be atoned, or paid for, before God. We must all, including the mothers, confess our sin of pride, and repent, turn around, so we can be forgiven. God hates the sin of pride. He exults in the humility of his children.

REFLECTION QUESTIONS:

1. Mothers, what example are you giving your children? Are you like a proud mother whose sons were called the Sons of Thunder by Jesus himself? Are you like a humble mom whose sons ruled a nation in humility and meekness?

2. If pride impacted mothers in such a way, what could pride do to you? How can pride impact a father? A grandfather or grandmother? A brother or sister? A child? How can cross-generational pride impact your family?

PRAYER

My dear heavenly Father,
Please protect me and my family from the sin of pride. Help us to walk in humility before you. I confess that pride has taken its toll on my family and myself. Please let me make atonement for pride through the sacrifice of Jesus, your son. I confess my pride and the pride of my family. I repent of being prideful. I want to turn around my life and go towards the direction where you are. Please give to me and my family the gift of humility.
In Jesus's name I pray. Amen.

CHAPTER THREE

ANGRY BIRDS

What is that shout? What is going on? It is the sound of birds coming at you. What a strange scene. We are beginning to panic! The birds are coming for us! The Alfred Hitchcock thriller *The Birds* never loses its effect upon the moviegoer. The birds, who are normally seen as nonthreatening creatures, turn on us. In our families, the birds coming for us, and at us, are agents of fear and death.

These birds are your children. These birds are angry . . . angry at you! Some parents have deflected any type of help because they are also angry. Other parents, by contrast, assume any type of help. These parents are also angry. All parents are angry. All children are angry. There is plenty of anger to go around. What do we do?

What we do is *stop*. We stop to see the birds. We stop to see the reactions, the results. We try to understand where all this anger is coming from. We stop. We do nothing.

We stop to see the birds, truly see them for who they are. These birds come at us in many conditions. They wear racetrack numbers, leotard skins, and the freaky Friday look. There's the funny and loving type, the unfunny and unloving type, the loaded after the day after, the sunny outgoing, the longing and remorseful, the constantly seeking type, the guessing-is-in-order type, ad nauseum, sui generis. They all pass by, and they are all angry. What do we do? We try to understand.

And we do nothing.

Anger is another sin that affects us and our children. Anger is also on the list of capital, or life-taking sins. Anger is a sin that drains us of energy and leaves us depressed and worn out. Anger is also called wrath and rage. Anger is "an intense emotional state involving a strong uncomfortable and non-cooperative response."[9]

Anger is defined by the American Psychological Association as "an emotion characterized by antagonism toward someone or something you feel has deliberately done you wrong."[10] Like pride, anger can be both good and bad. Anger can be good when it shows up as righteous indignation, but bad as uncontrolled rage. Anger is an emotion that builds up and either explodes outward or inward. Both are dangerous and destructive reactions. If you explode outward, you burn everything in your path. There is no controlled expression of outward anger. You explode. You say things that are hurtful and scorch the whole impacted terrain. If you explode inward, you become the willing victim of depression. Depression is anger turned inward. It is catastrophic for you. You burn inside while everything else seems to be going fine.

Anger also has a clock. An anger episode can happen in a moment, or it can seethe for a lifetime. Either way it is deadly. Anger is the only sin that kills its victim: you go fast in a burst or slowly in a seething burn. Anger is a very destructive sin.

In the Bible, we find a story of anger with far-reaching consequences. Told in 2 Samuel 13, this begins as a story about lust (a sin we will explore in another chapter), but anger is behind the scenes, creating chaos. Tamar, the sister of Absalom is presented to the reader as a beautiful young woman. Amnon, King David's oldest son and the heir to the throne, falls in love (lust?) with his half-sister Tamar and ends up committing incestuous rape against her. This is where the seemingly endless cycle of anger begins.

After all the plotting, posturing, and lying, Amnon rapes his half-sister but finds himself loathing her. His love for her turns to hate and this hate leads to anger. He throws her out, literally, and in his anger, he disowns her and humiliates her. Tamar is heartbroken and feels used and abused. She is also angry, but in her helpless situation this anger turns inward, and she becomes a desolate woman. She experiences depression and is left alone. Isolation is the worse treatment for depression. The Bible states that she lived in her brother Absalom's house in desolation, and we never hear from her again.

When King David hears of the episode, he too becomes angry, but for different reasons. Interestingly, the Bible is silent when it comes to a response to the incident from David himself. He did nothing. Nothing to discipline Amnon for his deed and nothing to minister to the needs of his daughter Tamar, who wallowed in deep depression. He did nothing about the great anger building up in his son Absalom. David could have been a positive influence in this situation and done everything in his power to calm down the storm of anger that had come to his family. But he did nothing. This theme, surprisingly, is unaddressed in the Bible. The story of David's anger just stops in the biblical narrative.

Many times, as parents, when we confront a situation of rampant anger, we do nothing. Our passivity comes as a result of having to face an overwhelming wall of anger and its consequences. We feel incapable of doing anything in the face of all the high emotions at play, so we do nothing. We have strong feelings for the well-being of our children, and these obscure the fact that anger should make us respond. We figure if we let this pass so everyone can come to their normal emotional state of being, all will be fine, and the emotions and anger will simply vanish. Not!

The biggest problem for David was about to unravel. His son

Absalom, who had a lot going for him, was deeply hurt and resentful by his brother's treatment of his sister. He was very angry but kept his anger bottled up for two years. Then he struck. He murdered his brother Amnon, the heir to the throne. His deep hatred for Amnon was made manifest when he murdered him. Amnon's anger toward his sister Tamar, whose anger toward Amnon turned inward, who angered Absalom to the point of committing murder, was quietly passed over by the anger of their father David. What a novella! ...

We can learn several lessons from this tragic story. First, anger comes because of bad decisions. Amnon had a great life. All he had to do was concentrate on being the next king. He had it in the bag. Instead, he chose to be tempted by the unreal desire to have sexual relations with his half-sister. While this type of incest was unusual at the time, he could have gone about this the right way and asked his father for her to be allowed to marry him. However, he did not want to marry her; he just wanted her for a one-night-stand. Instead, he listened to bad advice, lied, and made up a scenario that led to him raping his sister and then to unmanageable anger. This anger led him to dishonor his sister and throw her out of his house. The text tells us: "So Amnon hated Tamar with such intensity that the hatred he hated her with was greater than the love he had loved her with" (2 Samuel 13:15, CSB). He exploded with anger fueled by his hatred.

An interesting question that arises at this point is why Amnon had no remorse. He did not feel bad about the situation, nor did he feel any emotion toward his victimized sister. He demonstrated an immense amount of lack of responsibility for his actions. His pride showed up in his narcissism. His anger seemed to be the type that is "spur of the moment." You flare up, you explode, and then you go on as if nothing had happened. In his mind the incident was over. He made many bad decisions one right after the other without any thought of their impact on him, his father, his sister, or Absalom, his dangerous and deadly brother.

Second, for Tamar things were different. Where Amnon's anger ended is where hers began. She seemed to be a typical young woman with dreams and aspirations as the king's daughter. She anticipated the not-so-distant day when some dashing young man would come and marry her. She looked forward to the day she would be blessed with many children.

But in reality, she was required to take care of her sick brother. She liked Amnon and the conversations he had with her and others. She knew he would be king after his father, so she wanted to make sure he was happy. She went to his house to cook for him and minister to him as best she knew how. Instead, she was surprised to find that her half-brother wanted to go to bed with her. She told him to ask his father for permission to marry. (See 2 Samuel 13:12–14.)

Hebrew women saw chastity as their crowning honor.[11] She fought for her honor. She told Amnon, "Do not humble me" in the original Hebrew. She gave three powerful reasons why he should stop and consider his actions. First, she cited public opinion. Hebrew morality would not tolerate this act. Second, she stated that the act was wicked, and God would not approve. And third, this act would make him a fool.[12] Finally, she told him to ask the king for permission. He ignored her wishes and raped her. She then told him he could not throw her out but must deal with the consequences of his actions. He threw her out of his house by force. She reacted in anger and tore her clothes and sought out her brother Absalom (2 Samuel 13:18–20).

Tamar was the perfect victim. She did nothing wrong. She was the victim of sexual assault, and like modern research has shown, she knew who the predator was in her family.[13] Surprisingly, she was willing to follow through and be her brother's wife. She was willing to sacrifice herself and her wishes for his honor in public. However, she was scorned by Amnon and left alone—like a widow with no husband and children.

But this was unnatural for her, there was no wedding, no celebration. No one understands what a victim of rape goes through. She was innocent. Yet she fell, understandably so, to the pressure of the sins against her and became angry . . . and turned her anger inward. As a victim she desperately needed help. We now know that she could not blame herself for what happened. Still, there was no one to help her.

So Tamar chose to turn her anger inward. Granted, this was a tough situation, and she didn't have the maturity or the know-how to deal with this situation in her life. But she became a victim of anger as well. We do not know how the rest of her life fared, but we can safely speculate that hers was not a happy life.

Third, Absalom was a more sophisticated case of bad decision making. He was also surprised by the situation his sister brought to him, but his response was to delay. He told her sister to be quiet and let this one slide since Amnon was family (2 Samuel 13:20). This negative response was a different way to turn anger inward, and it actually made his anger fester. He did not talk with his father about this. He spent two years putting up with Amnon and thinking that his brother's time would come. And it did, when no one remembered what had happened except those involved. Absalom's latent anger caused him to make the flawed decision to take justice into his own hands and murder his brother, vigilante style.

Fourth, King David made the ultimate bad decision resulting from this situation. He was also surprised by the events and got quite angry. But he did nothing! The Septuagint, the Greek version of the Old Testament, adds the following to the text of verse 21: "But he did not grieve the spirit of Amnon, his son, for he loved him because he was his firstborn."[14] It seems that he is denying by his actions that any of this ever took place. Yes, Amnon is guilty of rape. Yes, Tamar is a basket case as a result. Yes, Absalom is angry. But David does nothing. His love for his eldest son supersedes the situation. Before God, his decision to ignore the situation is the worst of them all. He sets in motion the prophetic words of the prophet Nathan in the chapter preceding: "Now therefore, the sword will never leave your house [family]" (2 Samuel 12:10, CSB, word in brackets mine).

Anger moves people to do bad things. Lust and pride moved Amnon to rape Tamar, but it was anger that sent her away from him. Anger moved Tamar to get deeply depressed because she was helpless, and no justice was allotted to her. Absalom was enraged and murdered his brother Amnon. David was furious but did nothing. We see all these people getting angry and doing bad things as a result.

The effect of the cardinal sins in this situation was compounded. Lust and pride did their share to magnify the effect of anger. Anger resulted in a different response in the lives of each one of those affected by this anger. Anger's impact in the lives of Amnon, Tamar, Absalom, and David was magnified in their lives to the point of dismal consequences.

Have you ever had to deal with the snowball effect anger creates? Maybe in your home or your workplace, someone knows just what buttons to push to get you angry. Have you ever thought where that anger will take you? Have you ever thought about the consequences of your anger? Sometimes we think we can get angry and that is it. Sometimes we forget that anger can go on and on without our knowledge and affect other people in ways we never imagined.

We live in a time where whole generations of young people, the Millennials and generation Z, seem to be continuously angry. Many do not even know where this anger comes from. The anger is just there. The experiences that caused this anger are too hurtful to process and thus are buried in their subconscious. The brain has many ways of processing anger. Many are not healthy or helpful.

"Teenage anger is a thing of legend."[15] This sentence marks the opening words of an article on teenage anger. No surprises here. Anger and teenagers provide for an interesting pair of ideas at best.

> Finding healthy ways to process anger can be a challenge even for the most mature of adults, but for teenagers' biology creates an extra layer of difficulty. Though on the outside teens may basically seem like (and insist they are) grownups, their brains and bodies are still growing.[16]

Lauren Allerhand, a clinical psychologist at the Child Mind Institute, states: "The prefrontal cortex, which is the part of our brains involved in problem solving and impulse control, isn't fully developed until your mid-to-late twenties."[17]

> Adolescents are also flush with hormones like testosterone and estrogen, which can have a significant impact on mood. When kids make impulsive decisions or seem like they're overreacting to small provocations it can be helpful to remember that they're biologically less equipped to manage overwhelming feelings—like anger—than adults.[18]

So, for teenagers and young adults, the problem of anger is compounded by other factors such as biology and other global issues affecting everyone as well. These issues include "the ongoing fight against racial injustice, fears about climate change, and uncertainty about what the future holds."[19] So the issue of anger is exacerbated by the social issues we all confront and the situations they put us in.

Anger has long-lasting consequences. The chain reaction to anger affects everyone around it. Perhaps Amnon was the only one who thought the situation was done when he threw Tamar out of his house. Perhaps he thought Tamar would get over it and forget it. But he was wrong. He had set in motion a chain reaction and he had no idea where it would end. The anger began with Amnon, then Tamar, then Absalom, then David, then it leaped to a series of events that caused David to flee Jerusalem while running from Absalom, who was killed by Joab at the end. Everyone in that circle was impacted by the anger of Amnon, which radiated to impact other people around them.

All of this was the product of angry birds. These angry birds react irrationally to the situation and those around them. The final product is that the family system is left in shambles. So, the next time you get angry, look around to see whom your anger is impacting. Look to see how your anger is affecting your family. Look to see how anger is leading you to make a bad decision. Are you like Amnon, who goes on with life like nothing happened? Are you more like Absalom, who gets angry and seethes for years before he does something destructive to others? Are you like Tamar, who took her anger inward and experienced deep depression for the rest of her life? Or are you like King David, who got angry and did absolutely nothing to make the situation better? Whatever your situation, you need to deal with your anger now.

So which angry bird is your likeness? Have you ever been like Amnon, who loved, then hated, and in his anger, he exploded? Have you been like Tamar, a victim of anger that imploded and held everything in, living with depression? Have you been like Absalom, the one with the delayed angry reaction? Have you been like David, who even though he was angry, he did nothing? Which one describes you best?

Like Eli the high priest, and Samuel the prophet before him, David, the great king, failed in disciplining his sons. Today, so many men in positions of power have the same problem with their children. They are too busy with the public that they have no time to really deal with the private. These lapses in discipline have serious consequences. David found out the hard way. Time takes its time in making sure that all sin comes out, and its consequences.

As Robert Bergen points out in his commentary: "The sins of one generation imprint the next generation. Each sin not only fosters more sin, it also fashions it by providing precedents for others to follow."[20] So David set himself up for personal and family failure by doing absolutely nothing. Note that this was never David's original intent. This was a reaction to his sinful actions and their parallels. What he did impacted others around him in many ways. Anger, unmanaged, took care of the actions of his angry birds. This too can happen to you and your family.

Finding the answer to remedy the effects and results of anger is difficult. The only actions that will reverse the effects of anger are love and forgiveness. The wrong done must be forgiven. For forgiveness to occur, each wrong must be atoned for before God and man. The problem with David and his family is that they did not seek forgiveness. Forgiveness for the unrighteous deeds of man within man and forgiveness before God. David and his family members sought out neither. Their sin of anger was not atoned for at all. God would have forgiven them for their anger. God could have made them experience different results in this cycle. But they never said they were sorry for their anger. They never experienced peace.

REFLECTION QUESTIONS

1. How does anger affect you? Do you blow up and scorch your environment and those around you? Do you quietly take control and turn your anger inward?

2. How do you see anger affecting your children? Does their anger, and their response to anger, affect you? What do you do?

3. What bad decisions have you made because of anger? How would you change the situation so that anger is not the cause of the results?

4. When you get angry, do you seek forgiveness?

PRAYER

My dear God in heaven,
Please put a spirit of love and forgiveness in me and in my family. May anger never sink my family like it sunk the family of King David. Please let my family be kind and loving in all we do. I confess that I get angry and do not respond well. I confess that my family is angry and responds negatively as well. Please forgive us. Please show us your love in atoning for this sin. May the sacrifice of Jesus also cover and atone for this sin of anger.
I pray these things in the name of Jesus. Amen.

CHAPTER FOUR

LIVING ON THE LAZY RIVER

One of the most amazing creatures in the animal kingdom is the ant. From ancient times, this small insect has become an example of good time management and industry. In fact, the ant's behavior has become an example to countless generations of humans. Why? Because the ant embodies the antidote to the character failure we call sloth. According to Proverbs 6:6–11 one is told to go to the ant for a lesson:

> Go to the ant, you slacker!
> Observe its ways and become wise.
> Without leader, administrator, or ruler,
> it prepares its provisions in summer;
> it gathers its food during harvest.
> How long will you stay in bed, you slacker?
> When will you get up from your sleep?
> A little sleep, a little slumber,
> a little folding of the arms to rest,
> and your poverty will come like a robber,
> your need, like a bandit.

LIVING ON THE LAZY RIVER

The writer of Proverbs explains that without any institutional organization, the ant gathers food in summer for the winter. Then the writer turns to the slacker with an admonition to get up or you will be facing financial straits! The small ant demonstrates the need for doing the right thing at the right time. John Ortberg defines sloth as "the failure to do what needs to be done when it needs to be done."[21] Ortberg believes that the sin of sloth creeps very gradually into an unsuspecting life. The small and unassuming ant is an active example of how we should live and carry on.

By contrast, another one of the most interesting animals is the sloth. This is one of those unique instances where the name of the animal portrays one of its main characteristics: sloth. This animal seems to take forever to do anything. According to the World Wildlife Fund: "Sloths—the sluggish tree-dwellers of Central and South America—spend their lives in the tropical rain forests. They move through the canopy at a rate of about 40 yards per day, munching on leaves, twigs and buds. Sloths have an exceptionally low metabolic rate and spend 15 to 20 hours per day sleeping. And surprisingly enough, the long-armed animals are excellent swimmers. They occasionally drop from their treetop perches into water for a paddle."[22] Can you imagine moving only 40 yards in one day? Can you imagine taking a dip in the afternoon? Well, I can think of teenagers that would like to do that!

Sloths really live up to their name. Their curved claws allow them to hang like a hammock from a tree branch for hours without any effort on their part. These animals are hard to find in the forest canopy because they blend in naturally with their surroundings. Their slothfulness gives them the characteristic of unity within their context.

The sin of sloth is an interesting and unusual sin. This sin does not seem like a sin at all. In fact, the Bible rarely mentions it. How did this seemingly innocuous sin become one of the seven capital sins? A cautionary old English proverb states: Idleness is the parent of all vice.[23] I mean, who would deem a little relaxing as sin, right? This sin may not seem like much on paper, but the consequences of sloth lead to poverty and hunger, resulting in destruction and death, as the Bible can attest. (See Proverbs 14:23; 18:9; 19:15; and 24:30–34.)

Ironically, in our culture, the negative behaviors for this sin of sloth are held up and applauded as positive behaviors. For example, we are all familiar with video games. These are not bad in themselves, but our society deems as normal spending hours playing these games. The same goes for binge-watching TV series. One can easily spend hours a day binge-watching, and no one thinks this is bad. So we must look more carefully at this sin we call sloth.

Senior citizens are also prone to be captured by this smooth sin. One is actively working one day and goes into "retirement" the next. For many people this event happens when they reach the age of sixty-five. Suddenly, they stop. They quit doing what was previously on their list of habits. Then they slowly, over time, do less and less. Suddenly, the TV becomes more important in their lives. The internet and social media take a primary role, and soon they are addicted to these devices. Their diet changes. They are not interested in physical exercise anymore. They know the effects of this lifestyle will shorten their lives, but they continue being slothful. Many of them grow fat. (More about gluttony in a coming chapter.) Many start demonstrating the harmful effects of sloth in their health as it deteriorates. In less than a year they are lazily waiting for the day when they are called into God's presence. They have gradually become people that personify sloth.

What Is Sloth?

Sloth, or its most formal name of *acedia*, or more informal name, *laziness*, is defined in this fashion. *Acedia* comes from the Greek *akedia* which is derived from *a*, meaning "lack of" and , meaning "care." This "lack of care" has been defined as "a state of listlessness or torpor, of not caring or not being concerned with one's position or condition in the world."[24] In fact, acedia is thought by many people to be the ancient depiction of psychological conditions such as laziness, apathy, ennui, or boredom.[25]

Many psychologists see acedia as one of the primary causes of depression. The feeling of complete lack of care is the beginning of depression. One finds that one has lost the will or purpose for living life. Many people in their later years suffer from this psychological and spiritual problem. Many people die simply because they lost the will to live. This happens because they find themselves sitting in their living room with no purpose to fuel them.

So we have a potpourri of terms to choose from: acedia, sloth, laziness, laggardness, despair, negligence. These are all synonymous for the sin of sloth. Acedia, or sloth, is said to be "the thankless distaste of life, the general feeling of apathy and irritation arising from a low bodily tone."[26] The early monks described it as a heaviness or weariness of heart.[27] This symptom some of the elders described as the "midday demon" spoken of in Psalm 91.[28]

Not surprisingly, the demon of acedia holds an important place in early monastic demonology. Evagrius of Pontus (345–99 AD), a late fourth-century monk, characterized it as the most troublesome of eight genera of evil thoughts.[29] From early times in the church, acedia has been listed as a most grievous sin. But this sin is alive and well today just as it was in the early church. Yet no one takes it seriously.

Dante makes use of acedia in the *Divine Comedy* as the sin that leads him to the edge of hell to begin his descent into it.[30] This was Dante's big sin. It does not seem like a sin at all, but it opens the door for all other sins. This is indeed a horrible sin. But no one takes it seriously!

Chaucer also deals with this sin in his literature. For Chaucer, acedia includes despair, somnolence, idleness, tardiness, negligence, and laziness.[31] Does this ring a bell? Chaucer saw acedia as languishing and holding back. The lazy person refuses to take on the works of goodness because they are too grievous or too difficult to suffer. Acedia was the enemy of every source and motive for work.[32] Acedia is seen as an alienation from the world and then ultimately from oneself. It is a very bitter path to follow to the end. This is described as a state of restlessness, of not living in the present and seeing the future as overwhelming.[33] Now, who would want that for anyone in their family?

For retired people this sin is very deceiving. I must tell you that, surprisingly, even I almost succumbed to sloth. In my early sixties, I experienced a time where I was completely unemployed. My wife had already retired but we both felt there was more work and ministry for me down the line. We were financially stable, so I didn't need to work. I woke up when I wanted, I ate what I wanted, I did what I wanted, I went to bed when I wanted.

This seemed like the ultimate place of relaxation. This was true retirement! However, soon I was sitting in my La-Z-Boy thinking deeply about myself. I noticed how I was spending more and more time doing nothing. If you know me, you know I have never spent time doing nothing. In fact, my ADD dictated I do something, and then change to something else, so I did a lot in one day. I took long walks, but the desire to think and grow while walking was not there. I just walked. I used to read voraciously. Now I noticed I was barely reading my daily portion of the Bible and maybe one or two books I deemed interesting. I was reading little and more slowly. I also noticed that more and more I was spending time watching TV. These programs were a waste of time, and I knew that. In fact, I could not remember them nor did they build me up in any way, shape, or fashion. I was binging on my favorite programs. I was spending up to ten hours a day watching TV. I was a captive of sloth.

This seems unusual because a very productive person was suddenly on the sidelines doing nothing. I was wasting time. I knew it, but like an addiction I could not get rid of it. Ultimately, I came to the realization that I was a captive of sin. This sin needed to be atoned. I prayed to the Father to forgives me and change me into the productive person I had been and that I really was. God came through and my life was changed. I stopped being slothful.
So, what does this mean for you family? How does sloth show up?

In the Bible *acedia* appears a few times but with different names. The Old Testament warns of the results of laziness in the book of Proverbs many times, how it leads to destruction of self and others. (See Proverbs 12:24; 12:27; 18:9; and19:15.). The New Testament deals harder with this sin. In his parable of the talents, Jesus told how the master replied to the servant who hid the talent (money) he had given the man: "You evil, lazy servant!" (Matthew 25:26, CSB). And the master condemned the man for having done nothing with his money. Let us look in more details at this parable Jesus shared with his disciples a few days (in fact three days) before his crucifixion.

First let me give you a little context. Jesus was living his last week on this earth before his death and resurrection. But he was the only one, besides God, that knew the events to come. His disciples were completely in the dark. That Tuesday of Easter week, the disciples were in full mode for the Messiah's foretold coming. They knew something would happen, but they did not know what. Tuesday was a busy day for Jesus and his disciples. Jesus had just delivered his scathing denouncement of the Pharisees, Sadducees, and scribes. He had just looked at Jerusalem as they left the temple and were ascending the Mount of Olives and cried over the city. They were on their way back to Bethany, which is on the other side of the Mount of Olives.

On the way (Matthew 24:1), the disciples called his attention to the beautiful Herodian temple. And this set Jesus off on one of the longest of six discourses in Matthew. This passage is known as "the eschatological discourse of Jesus" or "discourse on the end times."[34]

Suffice it to say, Jesus's words shocked the disciples. They really were not understanding any of it. So he began to speak to them all that is recorded in Matthew 23 and 24. But let us focus now on one part of this discourse. It is interesting that Jesus, at the end of his time before the crucifixion, tells the disciples that one of the worst sins is laziness. He tells the story of a man who went away and gave each of his servants a sum of money. To one he gave five talents.

Now, let us take a minute to process this point. If you take the weight of a talent in gold as 60 minas, then a talent would weigh 1.25 pounds times 60 minas which equals 75 pounds.[35] If you use gold as the usual substance that made up a talent, then a talent was worth 75 times the price of a pound of gold today. As of this writing, a pound of gold is worth approximately $22,000. So we multiply by 75 and get the value of one talent in today's money, the amount of $1,650,000. The first servant gets five talents or $8,250,000. The next servant received two talents ($3,300,000), and the final servant received only one talent ($1,650,000). This should give us some perspective.

Then Jesus said the master comes back and called their accounts. The first servant told the master he doubled the sum, and now has $16,500,000! The master was overjoyed. He commended the servant and told him to share his master's joy. The second servant came forward to report that he also doubled his sum. He had made $6,600,000. The master responded in the same way as the first. He gave him congratulations and told him to enter in his master's joy.

Now the third servant is the one we want to look at in detail because sloth played a big role in his demise. This guy took the one talent and buried it! His reasons are not farfetched and very close to us. We might say he had common sense. He was not some Pollyanna type with his head in the clouds who was always thinking positive. He was a realist. He lived by the dictates of reason. He really knew his master.

He began his explanation to the master by telling him exactly that. "Master, I know you." And the truth is that he really thought he did. He told the master: "You are a harsh man, reaping where you haven't sown and gathering where you haven't scattered seed." He knew the character of the master. He knew the master was a hard man. He knew he was a self-seeker, so the master must also be a self-seeker. He knew this was a lose-lose situation. If he bartered and made an increase, then the profits would all go to the master and not to him. If he lost the money, then he would have to face an angry master who was predisposed to violence. Either way, he lost. So the third servant did the best thing reason dictated for him at the time: he hid the talent in the ground. Neither he nor his master would win.

And that was his first mistake. He thought he knew his master. He never really did. He never figured out that he was attributing falsely to his master this unloving hardness. He did not realize he was portraying himself as a liar. He never really knew the facts. Some commentators believe that here the servant was tacitly reproaching his lord for having given him too little to manage when compared to the others.[36]

So many times we think we can get in another person's head and figure it all out . . . mistakenly. We actually believe we are thinking for them and with them, that we know what they are thinking and feeling. Yet we get it all wrong from the beginning. My wife used to do this to me many times before I confronted her about it. She was acting like she knew what I was thinking! (So many wives do!) Thankfully, she stopped that behavior. Many people do that today. They believe they have "the gift" of thinking for others. They know what the other person is thinking.

Today one of the sins we see in families is people wrongly thinking for other people. Parents think for their children. Their children think for their elders. The grandparents think for their family members and others. This sin is bad because it creates a panel of lies and treats them as truth. Then people make key assumptions in relationships based on those lies. The servant had a relationship with his master. However, that relationship was faulty because the servant was looking at life in a mirror and not reality itself.

As if that was not enough, the servant then said: "So I was afraid and went off and hid your talent in the ground. See, you have what is yours." Why was he afraid? This is where we see the sin of sloth in action. He was afraid of paying a price for doing something he thought was disadvantageous to him. He was self-seeking and selfish, and he thought there would be no return for him in this transaction. So he chose to wait it out. He did nothing. He did not have to worry about it. He simply did not care. They entire time the master was gone, this servant did not have to bother with this responsibility. At the end, the money was there—nothing gained, nothing lost. Acedia won the battle.

LIVING ON THE LAZY RIVER

The master's response seems exaggerated. He seems to have made a molehill into a hill to die on. But when we examine the facts, we find out the real story and the dangers of sloth. The servant became unprofitable the moment he started selfishly to think for himself. For a master to have an unprofitable servant was unheard of at that time. The servant had squandered the one resource he had and the one resource he would never get back: time. In short, the servant had wasted not only his time but the master's as well. This was not good. For you see, you cannot go back and change time. All you have left is regret.

The servant paid dearly for his sloth. He was thrown into a lake of fire. He was disowned. We never find out if he had a family. We never find out if he had a job. All we know is that this sin overextended into all other areas of life and provided finality to his life.

Some people think of life as living on the lazy river. You just float and trust the current to lead you. Like Timon and Pumbaa, the funny characters of the 1994 movie *The Lion King* by Disney, and the song they made famous, you do not have to worry or care. Akuna matata![37] No worries! Why worry about things that are not in your control? Take it easy.

Well, you just may find yourself like my daughter when we went to a famous waterpark to spend the day. She was floating along lazily on the lazy river and then the inner tube flipped, and she hit the low bottom with her head and caused a ruckus at the whole park. She had scraped her head on the bottom and was bleeding. You cannot trust the river of laziness. This was a hard lesson to learn on a beautiful day!

Sloth can wreak havoc on your family very subtly. This is the one sin that opens the door to greater evils. As the saying goes: an idle mind is the devil's workshop. So many people get on this river and never seem to get off. Children today are experiencing relationships with their phones, their tablets, their computers, and other technologies. They seem mesmerized by the images they see. I like to say that they are "ikonized." Why go out and get sweaty and heated when you can experience life with this little machine? The river moves slowly, but surely, then ever so slowly, it swallows them. The years go by, and they find themselves isolated and helpless. They do not have the tools nor the experience to get this fixed. They have wasted their time, their parents' time, and our time. Yes, our time. We are all in this together!

Senior citizens get caught up with this sin as well. They slowly decide that they will do nothing. Nothing that is worthy of their time and effort. Soon they are victims to the perils of floating along the lazy river. Soon a disease like cancer overwhelms them. Soon the process of aging takes over and overcomes them. Soon they die . . . doing nothing.

You need to be proactive in your reactions. You need to be profitable. In other words, you need to redeem the times. What do I mean? All those projects you are putting on the back burner, not because they are sidetracks but because you do not want to deal with them at this time, need to come to the front. Speak to your son or daughter about their sexuality. Speak to them about their gender identity. Speak to them about their politics and policies. Speak to them about God. Speak to them about Jesus. Speak to them! Speak!

REFLECTION QUESTIONS

1. How is sloth showing up in your life? In the life of your family? What are you doing about it?

2. Do you have a "no cares, no worries" attitude like Timon and Pumbaa? Are you sure you are not letting acedia into your life?

3. Do you binge-watch TV programs? Why do you do it? Is it acedia creeping into your life?

4. How do you see the example of the servant who buried the talent?

PRAYER

My dear Father in heaven,
Please forgive us for not being at work. Please forgive the sloth in us. So many times, we flail aimlessly through life doing things that really do not matter. Please keep us working and busy for you. Let the sacrifice of Jesus Christ, your son, atone for the sloth that is so acutely affecting us. I am sorry for wasting so much time. Please let me find my purpose and that of my family.
In Jesus's name I pray this. Amen.

CHAPTER FIVE

LUSTY EYES

Come with me on a trip down memory lane to the time I was twelve years old. Like many kids my age at the time, I was an avid comic book reader. It just so happened that the comic book publishers knew that and inserted sundry ads for the strangest items in between the pages of my favorite comics. I remember reading with great interest an ad for "see-through glasses." Now, the appeal of these glasses came in that the person wearing them could see through concrete objects. Can you imagine? One puts on these glasses and then can see through everything! In fact, my mind gravitated to the picture in the ad: one could see through others' clothing! I quickly cut out the coupon, filled it out, and put it in the mail with the five dollars required for payment. (Scamming has not changed much!)

After endless days of anticipation, the US Post Office finally delivered my item. I was surprised by how small the envelope seemed but that did not deter me from opening it quickly. I took out the glasses (which were made from cardboard and plastic) and examined them—just cardboard glasses with rickety plastic frames. The lenses were cardboard with spiraling lines in red with a small hole in the middle to look through. I tried them on. Nothing happened. I figured you had to be in a real-life situation for them to work. I took them to school the next day. And some amazing things happened!

First, when I put on my glasses and started looking around, people started to look at me funny. But not funny, like, you are crazy, but funny, as in, why are you looking at me like that? People would cover their private parts or look the other way. This was strange. The glasses were really beginning to work.

Second, and even stranger, I started to really see through the clothes. I could imagine in my mind's eye what each one of them looked like without their clothes. This one caught me by surprise. I did not expect these glasses to work at all, and yet they did! I was looking at everyone without clothes. I figured why waste time on the uninteresting people and concentrate on the good-looking girls in my grade. I began to actively concentrate on them, and that is when things really got interesting. They began to squirm when I looked at them. They would turn and leave or else look at me and insult me for being a pervert.

Third, and really strange, is the moment when the assistant principal took notice of me and the situation I was causing. He ran to me and gave me a hard whack on the back of the head. He took off my glasses, grabbed me, and took me to his office, where I was to serve my detention. When I asked what I had done, he simply answered that I knew. When I told him it was just a cardboard lens in a plastic frame, he told me that was only half the story. The other half, he said, happened in my mind. It was for the second half I was being punished!

Jesus knew this was our natural state. If given the opportunity, our mind's eye or imagination would fill in the blanks intentionally, and sinfully. An innocuous cardboard lens with a hole in it could become a dangerous thing in the wrong hands. Any situation, regardless of how innocent, could become the stage for lust to shine. Jesus says: "But I tell you, everyone who looks at a woman lustfully has already committed adultery with her in his heart."[38] Here Jesus is not only defending the command against adultery, but he is giving us insight into the human psyche. He is defining lust.

Lust is a very complex sin. Someone said a long time ago that "lust is the craving for salt for a man dying of thirst."[39] So lust beckons man from the inside of his head with a very powerful desire to commit sexual sin. This desire is worthy of investigation.

What Is Lust?

According to a dictionary definition, "lust is a strong craving for sex."[40] This is a simple yet profound statement as written. It is simple because lust is the natural and fleshly boundless desire in humans to have sex. It seems that today's world seems to be ruled by this desire to copulate. The Bible refers to this necessary, and sometimes evil, desire as part of the compound we call the flesh. It belongs in the natural world and is by definition carnal. This is not heavenly stuff. Therefore, this desire, when unbounded, has been deemed a sin—something that misses the mark of God's will for our lives.

This concept of lust is also profound. How can something that seems so superficial and crass be so deep? Well, because it is rooted in the primeval evil that beset the world when mankind fell into the reality of sin in the garden of Eden. When Adam and Eve said to God that they were naked (Genesis 3:10), they gave the signal that something had broken. They were now able to "lust" after one another and even lust the things beyond.

How does lust sink your family?

Lust sinks your family in a subtle way, that eventually becomes public. This is a usually private desire that must come out in the open for it to be forgiven. If anyone in your family lets this wild animal out, there will be a price to pay. You have heard it said that "the grass is always greener on the other side." We will be talking about envy a bit later, but this adage applies to lust as well. Lust is always looking on the other side, seeking greener pastures. What lust does not know is that the grass is just as green on this side and without the hassle. There is no end to lust.

Lust never asks about the consequences of its actions. Lust looks, looks again, and keeps on looking till it fulfills its desire to conquer. In the Bible pages we have the story of someone who was led by desire, which led to some dreadful consequences. Yep, you guessed it, King David! (I knew you were thinking of Samson!) He was a model of spiritual virtuosity from his youth. He wrote some meaningful and deep psalms in his youth. He constantly looked for God's path in his wonderings. Yet the one time he let down his guard, lust was there waiting for him. His actions, guided by lust, led to his adulterous relationship with Bathsheba.

According to 2 Samuel 11, David was enjoying the brisk spring breeze that bathed his palace rooftop just in time to see the sunset. It was one of those lazy days when he slept his siesta without much on his mind. He had forgotten that his army was far away besieging Rabbah of the Ammonites. In fact, it was such a beautiful day that he forgot everything. He looked at the horizon as he walked, but to his dismay, there were buildings in the way. He looked down one of the rooftops and into the alley, into a backyard and, what do you know? He caught the image of a young woman bathing. She was a beautiful young woman, leisurely taking a bath, completely unaware of the lecherous and lusty eyes that were upon her. David was taken in by her beauty. Soon she finished her bath, and the show was over. This should have stopped David from continuing. But lust had ensnared him. He paced the rooftop with only one thought in mind: how to get to this young woman, or her body, that seemed to beckon to him. So he called one of his servants and inquired.

It turned out to be the young wife of Uriah the Hittite, one of David's best soldiers, and the daughter of Eliam, one of David's best fighters as well. Note that Eliam was the son of Ahithophel, one of David's best counselors, who ultimately betrayed him, probably because of this issue! (See 2 Samuel 15:31 and 23:34.)

David called Bathsheba to come to his palace and he slept with her. He was king after all. He could do what he wanted. Lust had its final completion indeed. Then David went back to normal as if nothing had happened. Clearly David's default for any sinful situation was to do nothing. (Remember how he did nothing about his anger either.) It seemed to David that God was not looking.

But that was not the end of the story. King David's lust then led to the murder of Uriah the Hittite at the hands of the Ammonites.[41] David then portrayed the benevolent king by marrying the widow, and set himself to await the birth of the new prince. The Bible tells us: "However, the LORD considered what David had done to be evil" (2 Samuel 11:27, CSB). God was watching!

Let's take a pause here and consider the panorama of the big picture. 1) David is God's chosen servant and model king. He is now around forty-five years old. He knows God and he knows the rules pretty well. He has memorized the ten commandments. He is at the top of his game. 2) Note that lust takes him down an easy path of temptation. He is leisurely taking a walk on his rooftop when he allows lust to lead him down a reckless path. He slid first into adultery and then into murder. Lust took his carnal desire to have sex with this young woman and brought him to his knees. He had to confess adultery and then murder. 3) Look at the results of uncontrolled lust: wanting and desire, adultery, lying, and ultimately murder. He thought no one was looking, but God was. All sin ultimately has its price to pay. God called him out. The Lord sent Nathan to David.

With two Hebrew words, Nathan called him out: "You yourself are the man!" This may well be the most dramatic sentence in the Old Testament.[42] David was a convicted man. Death was the penalty for adultery and murder. Lust had its way with him. Lust had proven its power to stand as a capital sin. But God is so gracious that he received David's contrition and repenting heart. He was pardoned, but with caveats. David's son, born as a result of sin, had to die. David cried and begged but to no avail. The baby died. So did the blessings of David's house. His sin put into play many repercussions that David did not want. Others in his family would pay as well. The sword would never depart his house. What a tragedy for a family.

What Can You Do about Lust?

As one can see from this tragedy in David's life, one can learn the general lesson that lust can be very dangerous for anyone. We live today in a world where lust is enthroned on high. Lust is the mover and shaker behind advertisements, dress, music, movies, games, and everything and anything. Lust is a powerful motivator in our world. Lust is everywhere. When you access the internet, lust is the face you see. Many advertisements and news are embedded with lusty messages and icons that promote temptation even for the strongest and most ethical of human beings.

Like David, we know the rules. Many of us know God. We even believe in Jesus. We think we have the Holy Spirit in us. Still, this is no guarantee that we won't easily fall into the temptation presented by lust. Like David, one can go down the river of life with lusty eyes to sexual destruction with lust leading the way, and never really take note of what is happening until the consequences come. Like David, the results of the fall can be devastating. Personally, and cross-generationally, the results are terrible.

For men in general, husbands in particular, lust is a dangerous enemy. Lust will easily tempt a man in a thousand ways on any given day. Lust is a continuous reality for a man. Lust, like it did to David, grinds away until it finds the moment where defenses are down. Lust looks for the time when spiritual pride and arrogance are enhanced. Lust teams up with pride and sloth to create a sinful situation. A married man will find one thousand outlets for his lusty eyes. The internet is a primary source. It provides privacy and license to follow lust down a slippery slope.

All married men know that adultery is wrong. And yet . . . lust beckons. Many a pastor or minister has had his demise thanks to giving in to lust in a weak moment. Pornography is viral and always at hand to help a fellow down. This is lust at its best. Lust takes a woman and objectifies her. Then lust takes this object and beautifies it to a superlative and sometimes unnatural degree. Then it takes the object and dangles it before lusty eyes. *Luxuria*, the Latin word for lust, evokes the nature of the pleasure. Yes, this can be yours. And thus so many men fall. This situation is alarming . . . and distasteful.

For wives things seem different, but are they really? Many wives become unsuspecting victims of lust. How are the tables turned? Ladies can fall in lockstep with lust thanks to all the fantasy plots around them and in their minds. There are myriads of books, online sites, reality shows, and real re-creations of fantasy that it is so difficult to stay pure. The private, and not so healthy, thoughts of women are sometimes taken over by lust. She may not fall into actually playing out those fantasies, but they are continuously in her mind. Lust rules her world. She may pretend to be happy in her life, but she really lives in another world.

LUSTY EYES

Lust takes over her habits, her dress, her conversation, her friends, and finally she falls head over heels into the temptation. Or not.

Many women suffer from chronic depression thanks to unfulfilled lives that lust has gutted from them. They do not think they are beautiful or attractive because they believe the lusty women are the real thing. They simply do not compare in their mind's eye. Thus they wrongly assume they are objects to be discarded or put aside. I dare say many unfulfilled women are victims of lust and do not want to publicly admit it. Women fall prey to lust just as much as men. The difference is how they fall.

Not surprisingly, our youth have become a battleground for lust. Lust has taken control of young people at alarming rates. The following study shows this point:

"Virtually every participant in this study, male and female, reported having experienced sexual desire—and they did so on a daily basis," concluded co-researchers Pamela Regan, a professor of psychology at California State University, Los Angeles, and graduate psychology student Leah Atkins. In their study, Regan and Atkins interviewed 676 men and women, whose average age was 25, on the intensity and frequency with which they experienced sexual desire. Almost all those interviewed—97.3 percent—reported having experienced lustful feelings, with men only slightly more likely to feel sexual desire (98.8 percent) than women (95.9 percent).[43]

Rampant sex is now the rage on the internet. You have phone sex, virtual sex, porn sex, casual sex, sex with friends, sex with strangers, and sex with a cherry on top. Young people are bombarded with lustful advertisements, dress, conversations, songs, literature, and even people dying for sex. They put out sex on their own and pay the consequences of premarital sex or else play with lustful fire and end up getting burned.

Our youth are easy prey to become lust's victims. Even young people who go to church are falling like dominoes. The odds are stacked against them. The physical changes in today's youth are no help. Not many years ago, a teenage girl getting pregnant was a tragedy. Nowadays, it's par for the course. Abortion has become the preferred method of contraception. The spiritual leaders at their worship centers are the last people to find out. The parents of the girl may never find out she was pregnant and that she aborted. No one keeps track of the guy who got the girl pregnant. It is her body, her baby, and her problem. Deadbeat dads are a tragedy of this generation.

Yet the real tragedy is with our children. Yes, our children! Lust is having a field day with them. They are given phones and tablets at younger and younger ages to keep them busy and entertained, and in turn they are led by lust to find dangerous entertainment that is unsafe for their young age or else they become the entertainment for others. Lust makes them the consumers or the victims of the sex-trapped world we live in. Scientists are doing little to help. "Lust clearly is deserving of much greater scientific attention than it has traditionally received."[44]

So what can you do? You can first, be informed. Be aware of the context you are in. Whether you are a husband, a wife, a single person, a young person, or a child, be aware. Be aware of your surroundings and of your friends. Be aware of opportunities for sin to happen. Be aware of people who want evil for you and your family. Be aware of God's gift of the pardon of sins and eternal life. Don't squander these; use them! You can stop lust dead in its tracks before it dismantles your world and sinks your family's ship.

REFLECTION QUESTIONS

1. What do you see in your life when it comes to lust? Do you see it in you? Do you see it in your family? Do you see it in those around you?

2. Look at your world. In your context, where do you see lust? Do you see it on the billboards around you? Do you see it on TV? Do you see it on the internet?

3. Are you a victim of lust? Do you look at a woman or a man "a second time"? Is someone in your family a victim of lust? What are you doing about it?

4. How are you protecting your family, your children, your spouse, your friends from being destroyed by the sin of lust?

PRAYER

My dear Father in heaven,
Please forgive my lust and the lust of my family. Please keep our eyes and our minds from this sin. Please guard me and my family from falling into the hands of lust. Atone for this sin through the blood and body of Jesus Christ, your son. I confess my lust and the lust of my family. I repent of this sin and seek the clean life you promised. In Jesus's name I pray this. Amen.

CHAPTER SIX

FATTER AND FATTER

Today we get to have our cake and eat it too. We live in a world where at least 50 percent of the population is likely to be overweight. More than half the world's population age five and older—51 percent, or more than four billion people—are projected to be overweight or obese by 2035, according to a report from the World Obesity Federation.[45] By comparison, 2.6 billion people worldwide (38 percent of the population) were overweight or obese in 2020.[46]

The problem is compounded in the United States. Here we really are a heavier country. Pastor Rick Warren tells the story of how he came to this realization. He was baptizing at a beach one day and he was overwhelmed by exhaustion. He was happy and joyful, but he felt tired. Then he realized that the people he was baptizing were mostly overweight. Furthermore, he realized he was overweight. This realization led to changes in him and in his congregation that began the Daniel Plan movement.[47]

In the United States, and other high-income countries, an estimated 60 percent of adults are overweight or obese.[48] These alarming results pale in comparison to what we are doing to our children, the real victims of our obesity. According to the State of Childhood Obesity, "roughly one in six youths have obesity, according to the newest available data. The data, from the National Survey of Children's Health, show that in 2021–2022, 17.0% of youth ages 10-17 had obesity."[49] We are teaching our children to be fat. We are literally fattening our kids for a dismal future!

According to *Forbes Health*, "obesity is defined as having a body mass index (BMI) of 30 or higher."[50] In other words, we are not talking about a person who is a little overweight. We are talking about people who are seriously overweight. Now, in the United States, you have the right to be fat and this right is protected by the government. You can be fat and your kids be fat, no big deal. But is this what God wants for us? Is something else operating on this front? Yes. The *sin* of gluttony. This is the sin that will eat itself out of a jam. This sin will really sink your family boat! Here is my story.

I never gave being overweight or obese a thought. I was always skinny while growing up. I ate whatever I had before me without giving it a care in the world. I got married and then our weight problem started. I say *our* because I dragged my beautiful wife into this pit. I am not proud of these actions, but they were the result of ignorance and negligence combined. At the time, my wife and I decided it was better for us to eat out than cook at home. Food was cheap then, so we ate out. Bad decision. In time, we methodically ate every item on the menu of several restaurants. Very soon we were both obese. Two bad results came out of this decision to be fat.

First, at sixty years of age, I had to do a total reset of my life. I was struggling with weight and high blood pressure. My weight had spiraled to a 265-pound high point. I managed to bring it down to 240 pounds, but it never dropped below that. I finally took my weight and health seriously and got down to 210 pounds with healthy dieting, exercising, support, and prayer. This was not easy. I still have 30 pounds to get to my ideal weight of 180. This journey has been difficult. Put 30 pounds in a sack and try carrying it around all day. The guilt . . . the tiredness . . . the pain . . . the sin.

Gluttony is a very subtle sin. It is defined generally as excess in eating and drinking. "Gluttony (Latin: *gula*) is overindulgence and overconsumption of anything to the point of waste. The word derives from the Latin *gluttire*, meaning to gulp down or swallow."[51] This is a subjective definition. Gluttony for one person is not for another. It is difficult to gauge this sin. Nowhere in the Bible does it say that fat, or obese, people are cursed or sinful. Being fat has little to do with this sin. In fact, skinny people can practice gluttony. "Although eating and drinking for pleasure is not seen as sinful, eating or drinking to excess beyond reason is a sin. Drunkenness, which is caused by excessive consumption of intoxicating beverages, is considered a type of gluttony. As a deadly sin, gluttony is believed to spur other sins and further immoral behavior."[52]

Many people, in fact, do not see it as a sin at all. It is not in the decalogue of the ten greatest sins. The Bible refers to gluttony sparsely and never by name. No one is preaching today that gluttony is a sin. But it is. The fact is, the Bible condemns it in subtle ways. The book of Proverbs speaks against it: "Do not carouse with drunkards or feast with gluttons, for they are on their way to poverty, and too much sleep clothes them in rags" (Proverbs 23:20–21). In Ezekiel 16:49, we find that one of the great sins of Sodom named in God's judgment upon it was gluttony. Sodom's sins were pride, gluttony, and laziness, while the poor and needy suffered outside her doors.

Surprisingly, Pope Francis has taken on the challenge of preaching on the sin of gluttony on numerous occasions. He faulted gluttony in his commentary on world hunger, food insecurity, food waste, the obesity epidemic, and materialism. "During his Christmas Eve homily in December 2018, he called on Christians to forgo greed, gluttony, and materialism and instead focus on the holiday's meaning of love, charity, and simplicity."[53]

Simply put, the sin of gluttony is another form of idolatry. It is a personal choice to self-love, comfort, and control through food.[54] "Gluttony is the sin of overindulgence and excessive greed for food. In the Bible, gluttony is closely linked with the sins of drunkenness, idolatry, lavishness, rebellion, disobedience, laziness, and wastefulness."[55] Gluttony is addictive. The Bible takes gluttony very seriously . . . we do not.

In Eden, in the beginning of time, man and woman were confronted with a choice. The decision before them lay in whether or not to disobey God and eat from the fruit of the Tree of Good and Evil. According to Genesis 3:6: "When the woman saw that the fruit of the tree was *good for food* and pleasing to the eye, and also desirable for gaining wisdom, she took some and ate it. She also gave some to her husband, who was with her, and he ate it." (NIV, emphasis mine). Notice that the first thing that stuck out to Eve was this was good food. She was enticed by the fruit's desirableness. She ate and gave to her husband to eat, which he did . . . gladly. Gluttony seems to be, almost naturally, on the stage for the enactment of that very first sin. It comes so easily.

It is easy to put on weight, quite difficult to take it off. Just ask anyone trying to lose weight. The stigmas that come with being obese are not just unflattering but also ugly. You laugh at the fat jokes but knowing they are talking about you. You catch a private, not so private, conversation and find out your weight is the topic.

So at the end stage of my life, I realized how wrong I had been. I was convicted. I had sinned. God forgave me. But I still had to pay the consequences of my sin of gluttony. I am still paying.

The second negative result of my gluttony is what I had done to my children. This was inexcusable. My three kids grew up in a wholesome atmosphere in a home with Christian values. We always looked out for the best projection in life. We wanted all three to succeed in whatever they chose to do in life. We participated in sports and school activities. We taught the important things in life. We did not do one thing: watch their weight. Soon, all three kids were obese. And we were happy.

That happiness soon came to an end when they reached their adult lives. It causes me great pain to talk about this. The little one woke up one day and decided he would manage his weight. He wanted to go into the military, which had strict standards for weight. He placed himself on a low-calorie plan and only drank water. Soon he was losing weight and keeping it off. This one made it.

But the other two still struggle with this problem. Our society accepts it, but the individual usually does not. You know when you are overweight you are not happy. You can pretend, but one day you wake up. Something inside you tells you that you had enough.

Physically, the change is drastic. Being overweight impacts all our physiological systems. The heart and circulatory system begin to feel the pain of high blood pressure. It is no surprise to learn that this symptom is the silent killer. Your respiratory system begins to fail you, and you start wheezing after a short dash. Your structural systems begin to groan when you do the smallest physical effort. Your body begins to live in a mortal pain!

When you are young you can bear the weight, but with age comes the health consequences of obesity. The reports of "blue zones" in the world are now attesting to this fact. In the five traditional blue zones, long life expectancy of centenarians is a common fact. Many studies seek to discover the various reasons for this effect. However, one of the constants in these centenarians in blue zones is a healthy diet. Another is a lifestyle that makes movement a priority. A surprising benefit to do with the "spiritual" nature of their lifestyle. They have found a purpose and are content.

Gluttony means thinking and believing there is never enough. That resources will run out, so you need to eat now for tomorrow. Gluttony is an empty space that can never be filled, no matter what you eat or how long you eat it. Like Augustus in the movie *Willy Wonka and the Chocolate Factory*, gluttony never satisfies your desire for more.

The sin of gluttony is compounded in the family. The transgenerational passing on of the sin of the fathers became a reality with the sin of gluttony with us. The person who controls the diet of the family controls the health and future of the family. I was in control, and in my world, food was allowed as an available commodity for all to partake to its unexamined extent. My sin, unfortunately and unknowingly, became their sin. I am getting out, but they are still in this life for an unprescribed future . . . and I am convicted. They are beginning to see this is not good.

The Bible has a subtle take on gluttony. While considered one of the seven major sins of all time, gluttony is almost on the backdrop of the biblical sin lineup. "Gluttony, biblically speaking, can be summed up as laboring 'for the food that perishes' (John 6:27). It is not only found in over-consumption, but an idolatrous expectation that looks to eating and drinking to provide sating and fullness for the soul (inner person)."[56]

Please note that all food is provided by God to humans for their enjoyment. And I repeat: "A person's weight or physical appearance may have nothing to do with the sin of gluttony. Not all fat people are gluttons, and not all gluttons are fat."[57] Gluttony is the perversion that goes beyond the need to survive through eating to the need to satisfy some craving in the mind that cannot be sated. This anxiety drives the eater to overcompensate their usual and habitual eating patterns. The psychological drives the physical. Gluttony starts in the mind and not the stomach. As such, it cannot be dealt with unless one deals with the mental and emotional needs first. This always calls for a spiritual solution to the problem.

I have noticed three things we need to understand and overcome to combat and be victorious over gluttony.:

1. Gluttony is a mental need that seems to be only satisfied physically. This is why so many people characterize gluttony as a sin of the flesh. The reality is that gluttony, like all other sins, starts in the mind. Lisa Kutolowski has written a great article on this topic presenting the situation, the struggle, and the results.[58] She talks about her struggles, using a latte as an example. Her mind starts thinking about the latte and soon she is salivating and doesn't stop until she has bought and consumed a latte. This is how gluttony works, starting with the mind.

Thus, gluttony must first be fought in the mind. Dealing with the physical consequences first will lead one to the valley of despair. You must ask God to clear your mind so you can deal with this sin effectively. Like all these seven sins, it begins and ends with the mind.

2. Gluttony never has enough. It is never sated. You will eat and eat and eat, and you will never feel full. Of course, the downside of gluttony is that you will put on weight. Obesity is one of the end results of gluttony. You will become fatter and fatter. Or not. Conversely, you could be pulled into the vortex of bulimia. You will engorge and then go spit it out or vomit whatever you ate. This becomes an addiction.

According to Jason Liske:

> "Gluttony is never being quite content with what we have, always wanting more (not in the sense of greed, on which I shall speak later), filling not only our stomachs but our entire lives with excess and still wanting more. It bloats and distracts the soul, causing us to form idols out of things we think we "need", and helps us avoid reality by filling our lives with distractions (think shopping or eating as a "cure" for sadness). What we actually need has been replaced by want we think we need; what we think we want."[59]

So how can we stop getting fatter and fatter? The answer may surprise you in its simplicity: *stop!*

3. Gluttony can be solved by asking God for forgiveness and starting again. Only he can satisfy the cravings of your soul. Stop where you are. Stop and ask for forgiveness for the sin of gluttony, and allow God to change those habits that are pulling you down. Start with asking God to change one habit at a time. Think about what you are eating. Think about why you are eating. Change the negative habits and supplant a positive habit in its stead. With God you have the victory in sight.

REFLECTION QUESTIONS

1. What is your first thought when you think of gluttony? Is it positive or negative?

2. Have you ever had to deal with gluttony personally? Was it for a situation affecting you or affecting others? How did you respond?

3. Will you *stop* and ask God for forgiveness? Will you ask God to help you start again? See yourself as winning this battle in your mind's eye.

PRAYER

My Father in heaven,
Please forgive the sin of gluttony in my life and in the lives of my family members. Please cleanse my mind so that my body can be cleansed as well. May the sacrifice of Jesus Christ atone for the gluttonous desires in my life. I confess that gluttony has taken over a large part of my life. I repent of all the things I did to keep this sin alive in my life. Please restore my life to health and wholeness.
In the name of Jesus, I pray this. Amen.

CHAPTER SEVEN

THE WORLD IS NOT ENOUGH

Some people will try to get the most out of life by any means possible. For them the world is not enough. They desire everything and anything: they want it all! They soon find out the end of their folly: the world is more than enough. Greed, or more formally avarice, is a powerful and sinful motivator. We have already discussed that all sins begin in the mind. This one is no exception.

Imagine for a moment that you just graduated from high school. You have your diploma, all your relatives are congratulating you, you take all the pictures, you open your graduation gown to catch some air, and you look vaguely into the future. As you stand and gaze looking beyond the gateway of time into the future, a million voices yell at you, telling you, "The world is not enough. Go for it all! No matter what you have right now, it is not enough; you need more." You will always need more. The more you have, the more secure you will be. The more you have, the happier you will be. Why buy four rolls of toilet paper when you can buy forty-eight? Just think what you can do with ninety-six rolls! You will never have enough.

If you are like most Americans, this is what you hear. A million voices all telling you that the future is not enough. That whatever you

THE WORLD IS NOT ENOUGH

get is not enough. That there is always going to be more out there. But more of what? Can you ever be happy looking for more? Is more even attainable in this life? Let me share with you three directions that will speak truth for whatever path you take.

1. The first direction takes you into the world of reality. The reality of greed. You will find that greed is a constant in our lives . . . our whole lives. Greed is also known by the older names of avarice, covetousness, and ambition. Now, some people see a positive side to ambition. They believe that ambition, focused on the positive, is a good thing. For example, if you are ambitious to help other people, then that is good. This is a topic for debate, but we will not address it here.

So how do you define greed? According to yourdictionary.com, greed is "an excessive desire to acquire or possess more than what one needs or deserves, especially with respect to material wealth."[60] Vocabulary.com goes a little further and deeper in its explanation of the term, calling it ugly and insatiable, and giving us the etymology of the word. "Greed comes from the Old English *graedig*, or 'voracious' which means 'always hungry for more.'"[61] I can sum up greed in six words from the vocabulary of a two-year old: want want; gimme gimme; more more!

Do you want to be rich? Everybody wants to be rich today. No one sees any problem in reaching into the cauldron of the world's riches to get their hands on the prize. We will take great risks, and I mean really risky stuff, for the promise that one day we will be rich. Just ask anyone with a gambling problem or addiction. The great psychologist E. Stanley Jones once said there are two ways to be rich: own everything or want nothing. There is a great deal of truth in that statement.

Unfortunately for us, greed is a sin that also crosses the generational divide. Greed is a great danger to you and to your children and their children. It is a highly contagious and immoral virus that refuses to go away. It stays in the backdrop of our minds throughout our lives and the lives of our family members. Vladimir Putin is the latest incarnation of this virus called ambition. Just think for a minute, Putin has everything he always wanted and then some. What is he worried about? What keeps him up at night? What does he want?

Simply put, he wants more. One just need look at pictures of the destruction of Mariupol in Ukraine to see the extent that one man's ambition will lead to today. Greed leaves a wake of destruction in its path. How much is enough? This is how all wars impact us. How much is enough destruction and pillage? Greed is the motivation behind most wars.

2. The second direction takes you into the biblical world. The Bible gives many examples of the biblical teaching on greed. This is why it should not surprise us that the Bible deals harshly with greed. In fact, this is the reason why greed, or covetousness, or avarice, is one of the seven capital sins. The Bible provides many examples of the sin of greed and its punishment. For starters, you have the people of Israel in the desert. God gave them at Sinai the "ten words" to live by in this world in a godly manner. The tenth commandment is a condemnation of greed. In Exodus 20:17 you find the following words: "*You must not covet* your neighbor's house. *You must not covet* your neighbor's wife, male or female servant, ox or donkey, or anything else that belongs to your neighbor" (emphasis mine).

Covetousness, or greed, is not a pretty thing. Proverbs 1:19 gives a resolute statement of the result of greed: "Such is the fate of all who are greedy for money; *it robs them of life*" (emphasis mine). Truly greed robs people of their lives. This is exactly what happened to Ananias and Sapphira in Acts 5, literally. They had sold an inheritance and got greedy with the profits. They took out a part of the profits for themselves and lied about it to Peter the apostle. He asked them individually, to see if they rectified their mistake, and they did not. So Peter condemned them for lying to the Holy Spirit, and then they both died. Wow! Their greed literally robbed them of their lives!

Jesus spoke clearly against greed. In fact, that is the main point of his parable, or moral teaching, on the rich fool. Greedy people, according to Jesus, are foolish people. In Luke 12:13–24 we find this parable and its commentary by Jesus. The story begins with a petition. It seems someone in the crowd that day was looking for the rabbi to pronounce judgment over a brother's greed. This was probably a younger brother complaining about the legal takeover by the oldest brother of the whole estate of their father. Jesus stepped out of the way and made a pronouncement against greed. "Then he said, 'Beware! Guard against every kind of greed. Life is not measured by how much you own" (Luke 12:15). Jesus then told the crowd a story to amplify and explain his teaching on greed.

The tale begins with a rich man whose business was doing very well indeed. He said to himself, "What should I do? I don't have room for all my crops." Now this is a good problem to have, to have done so well that you do not have enough space to warehouse the surplus. Many of the world's wealthy citizens today are billionaires. Do you know what a billion is?

Then the rich man said, "I know what I will do. I will tear down my old warehouse and built a nice new warehouse." Then he said to himself, "Buddy, you have enough laid up for years! So sit back, relax, eat, drink, and live it up!"

But God said to him, "You fool! You will die this very night. Then who is going to get everything you worked for? Not you!"[62]

Jesus concluded his teaching by saying, "Yes, a person is a fool to store up earthy wealth but does not have a rich relationship with God" (Luke 12:21).

In his Sermon on the Mount, Jesus again spoke out against greed. He told the people: "Don't store up treasures here on earth, where moths eat them and rust destroys them, and where thieves break in and steal. Store your treasures in heaven, where moths and rust cannot destroy, and thieves do not break in and steal. Wherever your treasure is, there the desires of your heart will also be" (Matthew 6:19–21). Basically, Jesus cautioned the people not to be greedy with the goods of this earth that are perishable, for our treasure reflects what is in our heart. This serves to remind us that in the Bible, greed, or covetousness, is considered a serious sin.

Leo Tolstoy, the great Russian novelist, wrote a short story in 1886 titled *How Much Land Does a Man Need?*[63] In brief, this is the story of a man called Pahom. The Bashkirs, a humble clan of farmers, agree to sell to Pahom, for the ridiculous amount of one thousand rubles, all the land area he could walk around, or encircle, in one day. Pahom started walking very early and marking his territory with his spade. He got greedy and walked and walked until he realized the sun was about to set. He ran back to the starting point as fast as he could and arrives just as the sun was setting. The Bashkirs cheered his good fortune, but to their surprise, Pahom dropped dead. He was buried in a grave that was six feet long and two feet wide, answering the question posed by the title of the story.[64]

How much land, money, resources, power, toilet paper, do you need?

3. The third direction gives us the antidote for greed. Greed can be overcome and conquered with contentment and generosity. Contentment is the virtue that results when one is happy with what one owns or with the situation one is living. The perfect example of contentment in the New Testament is the apostle Paul. He wrote to the Philippian church: "I know how to make do with little, and I know how to make do with a lot. In any and all circumstances I have learned the secret of being content—whether well fed or hungry, whether in abundance or in need. I am able to do all things through him who strengthens me" (Philippians 4:12–13, CSB). Contentment is the antidote for greed.

The opposite of greed is generosity. Generosity is the virtue of compassion that supplies the needs of others by giving away one's own resources. Both virtues, together, will kill the virus of greed. This same dynamic can operate in your family. When you are content with what God provides and generous in giving to others in need, then God supplies your every need and crowns you with many blessings. Content and generous parents will always result in content and generous children. This pattern will self-perpetuate for generations and generations.

Sadly, the opposite is also true. And even sadder, the norm for people today is for greed to rule their lives. When greed rules your life, then your family will suffer as well. And the pattern will replicate for generations. So, how do we stop the onslaught of greed?

We find the perfect example of transformation of this kind in a man called Zacchaeus. (See Luke 19:1–10.) You know the story. Jesus met Zacchaeus in Jericho when the man climbed a sycamore tree to get a better view of the Jesus parade. Jesus called him down and visited at his home. Zacchaeus was transformed from being a greedy little man to a content and generous disciple of Jesus.

What about you? How greedy are you? How much do you need?

Here I must interject my testimony. One day I was driving down Ocean Drive in Miami Beach next to the Hilton Fontainebleau hotel and the huge yachts on the intracoastal waterway, beside the monster mansions on the other side. I loudly complained to God. I was making peanuts as a pastor, and I could have been a megarich lawyer instead. God then reminded me of the last temptation of Jesus. Not the movie, the text in Matthew 4. The last temptation was greed. The call of ambition to rule the world. God reminded me that he would take care of me and give me more than I could imagine. Today I am an incredibly blessed man. Even though I am materially blessed, the reality is that I am content with what I have. I am rich because I want nothing. I have everything I need.

Greed can quickly sink your family. Greed can rob your family of the things that matter. Greed can easily be transferred from generation to generation. Greed is for fools.

Nevertheless, this capital sin of greed was atoned for as well by Jesus. If you pray and trust Jesus with your life, you will experience true contentment. This will not only affect you but also will be the trademark for your children and theirs.

REFLECTION QUESTIONS

1. Are you a victim of greed? Do you long for the things that you wish you had?

2. Are you like Pahom in that you are trying to get the most you can? What are your thoughts on the afterlife from the point of view of the rich fool?

3. Are you content with what you have? Are you content with what you do? Are you content with your family members?

PRAYER

My heavenly Father,
Please cleanse my life of all greed. Give me the blessing of contentment in my life so that I can be sated by the things I have. Help me remember that there is always a brother or a sister who has a greater need than I do. Help me to imprint my children with the gift of contentment so they can share this blessing as well. Thank you because Jesus atoned for this sin on the cross of Calvary.
In Jesus's name we pray this today. Amen.

CHAPTER EIGHT

THE NEIGHBOR'S GRASS

For Father's Day, not too long ago, I decided to preach about envy and how it affects the fathers in our midst. Envy seems like an off topic for Father's Day, but the truth is, we all must deal with the realities we face. Envy is particularly detrimental for the family when the father is the agent of this sin. Envy in fathers is quite common. The problem is when it is downloaded to the rest of the family, envy can cause lasting damage.

Proverbs 14:30 is an admonition against envy, or its identical twin sister, jealousy. The writer of Proverbs writes: "A tranquil spirit revives the body, but envy is rottenness to the bones" (NET). Some translations translate jealousy for envy in this verse. Envy can really create havoc in the life of a man.

The Bible tells the story of a man who had to deal with envy, but did so in the wrong way. He knew what God wanted but let someone else fulfill his dream, and so envy had its way. The punishment meted out not only impacted him but his wife and children, in the most negative way. Envy never got to impact most of his grandchildren because they were never born. Seventy of his sons were put to death by the leaders of the town after he was gone. (See this story in 2 Kings 10:1–8.)

That man was King Ahab of Israel. In the Bible we discover how envy led to this destruction of his life and his family. In 1 Kings 21:1–29 we find the beginning of his story. Ahab saw the vineyard of Naboth and wanted it. I mean, he *really* wanted this vineyard. So he went to Naboth and asked him to sell him the vineyard. Then he conveyed his terms. Convenience was one reason Ahab was so intent on the purchase. He wanted the vineyard for a vegetable garden because it was right next door to the palace. He told Naboth he would find him a better vineyard, or he would pay the price of the vineyard in silver. Naboth did not budge an inch. He told Ahab this was his paternal inheritance. He would never sell it in a million years.

Ahab returned home dejected and upset. He didn't eat. He moped around wishing for his dream vineyard to materialize someway somehow. And then his wife, Jezebel, the daughter of a pagan king, came to him and asked why Ahab was so down. He responded that Naboth turned down his offer for the vineyard. Jezebel laughed, and then reminded him that he was king in Israel. She told him she would take care of the problem. And she did!

She wrote letters in Ahab's name to the town leaders, telling them to proclaim a town fast and accuse Naboth of being a traitor. She instructed them to find two false witnesses to bear claim against Naboth that they heard him curse God and the king. They did all they were told. They believed the orders came straight from the king! Naboth was quickly found guilty and stoned outside the city. Then Ahab took over the ownership of the vineyard for free. Naboth's sons were completely out of the picture in this title transfer. This was a strange enough situation at the time, but so were Ahab's sons and grandsons.

Then the prophet Elijah appeared. God directed him to go to Samaria and pass judgment upon Ahab and his family for the sins of envy and murder against Naboth. In short, Elijah told the king that God would "bring disaster on you and will eradicate your descendants: I will wipe out all of Ahab's males, both slave and free, in Israel" (1 Kings 21:21, CSB). Jezebel was also punished, but that is a story for another day. The account of Ahab and Naboth is a classic tale of envy and its power to destroy families.

Let's focus on the cardinal sin of envy and learn a few truths about this final sin in our list of seven.

First, envy is an optical problem. Different sins begin in different places. Envy always begins with the eyes. You see something and compare it to what you have. Then the results come in. *Envy* derives from the Latin *invidia*, which means "non-sight." Envy is when you decide that what someone else has looks better than what you have.

Envy will make you unhappy. How? By creating discontent with your current life. Envy makes you desire things beyond your reach, and you do everything in your power to get what you want. Still, you are never satisfied, never happy.

Envy is defined as "painful or resentful awareness of an advantage enjoyed by another joined with a desire to possess the same advantage."[65] This painful awareness sealed the fates of both Ahab and Naboth. They were both victims of envy. Ahab was the perpetrator who fell on the sword of envy. Naboth was the victim of Ahab, who had the sword of envy fall on him. The ending was terrible for both!

This reality leads us to a second truth.

Second, envy is a spiritual problem. Envy begins with the eyes but quickly moves to the heart, where it becomes a spiritual issue. Envy takes a sin of the flesh and makes it a sin of the spirit. For when you envy someone for something that person has (which is usually the case), you fall into a dangerous wormhole that transports you quickly from the earthly realm to the spiritual realm. How?

Envy denies the wisdom of God. I know what is best for me, not

God. Envy denies the provision of God. God does not really care for me. Envy denies the judgement of God. God does not care what I do. Envy denies the power of God. God could not do better for me in this life. Envy denies God's supremacy in your life. I know more than God.

These realities place envy head and shoulders above the other sins. So why do humans do this all the time? Well, there is a reason for that. Ralph Waldo Emerson, the American philosopher and educator, said: Envy is ignorance.[66] I would tend to agree. Envy is ignorance of God and ourselves. This reality is blatantly evident in Ahab's story. He was ignorant. He had no idea of the repercussions of his envy. He had no idea how it would affect his legacy. He had no idea how it would affect all his family. This brings us to a third point.

Third, envy is a family problem. Like the other six cardinal sins we have discussed, envy can sink your family, by creating discontent in you. Envy, and its results, are transmitted to your family members as well. They also become discontented with what they have. In fact, they may look at you and envy someone else who could take your place. For example, my wife could very well compare me to someone else's husband and want to replace me with a better model. Easy divorce. Incompatible differences? Nah, I shopped and looked and found a better model.

Another example taken from today's teenagers: "I hate my family. I wish I had a family like so and so. Their parents are cool. Mine are a drag." You get the point. Envy is sinking our families in a major way. This sin is difficult to overcome because in our materialistic culture, this sin is prevalent. Envy rules.

Ahab and his family were destroyed by envy. The repercussions of one sinful and envious act can send a family spiraling down the eternal abyss. Ahab's family all came to a violent ending thanks to one envious act. The envy of Ahab led to the murder of Naboth and the stealing of his vineyard. This act had serious repercussions.

So how can we overcome envy? The solution is contentment and trust in God. When you are satisfied with what you have, you will never be tempted to look at the false greenery on the other side. The Bible shares with us the great example of contentment we find in life of the apostle Paul. He was living, or better yet existing, in a Roman prison. He was chained for most of the day and probably the night. He had very few things to call his own. He had been left high and dry by his friends who seemingly forgot him. In the middle of all of this, he writes to the Philippian church: "I know how to live on almost nothing or with everything. I have learned the secret of living in every situation, whether it is with a full stomach or empty, with plenty or little. For I can do everything through Christ, who gives me strength" (Philippians 4:12–13).

Paul had truly found the secret to defeating envy. He knew Jesus Christ had atoned for that sin on the cross at Calvary. Jesus resurrected so he could live in strength and the hope that there would be a better day. He did not have to envy anyone for anything. He had all he needed. Not just for that day but for forever!

When we fail and sin and envy has its way with us, the surprise is that God is always willing and ready to be compassionate to the penitent. Repentance is always the first step back to normalcy and back to God. The story of Ahab has a very interesting and surprising ending. Ahab repented. "But when Ahab heard this message [a terrible message of doom for his family], he tore his clothes, dressed in burlap, and fasted. He even slept in burlap and went about in deep mourning" (1 Kings 21:27, words in brackets are mine).

Ahab understood what he had done and repented. God saw it and was compassionate. God will honor all true repentance. God said to Elijah: "Do you see how Ahab has humbled himself before me? Because he had done this, I will not do what I promised during his lifetime. It will happen to his sons; I will destroy his dynasty" (1 Kings 21:29). With God, hope is always a reality! Repentance will always be well received. The sacrifice of Jesus covers and atones for *every* sin, all the time, anywhere!

REFLECTION QUESTIONS:

1. Do you see Ahab in yourself? Do you have everything that you need but you think you are missing just one thing? What is your vineyard?

2. Have you thought about the consequences of envy in your life? In the life of your husband or wife? In the lives of your children?

3. Are you willing to come to terms with God over the sin of envy? Are you willing, like Ahab, to repent and start again?

PRAYER

My Father in heaven,
Blessed be your name! Please guard my life from the cardinal sin of envy. Lord, guard my eyes so I do not look at the blessings of others to want them. Protect my family from falling under the curse of envy. I confess to you the times I have been envious. I repent of my envy. Please pardon me and cancel my consequences for this sin. Thank you because Jesus atoned for this sin on the cross of Calvary.
In Jesus's name. Amen.

CHAPTER NINE

ESCAPING CAPITAL PUNISHMENT

How does God discipline his kids? How does God see these seven capital sins and how does he respond when we commit them? To find out let us look in the Bible at the book of Numbers, chapter 32.

In the passage we read about the issue Moses had with the tribes of Reuben and Gad. The eastern side of the Jordan had been won in war. The two tribes wanted to settle down in that area and not help with the rest of the conquest. Moses told them that was not an option. They gave Moses another option, which God approved. The two tribes would settle in the land they wanted *but* they would send their men fully armed in front of the other tribes when they went up to conquer the Promised Land. After agreeing with their terms, Moses gave them a stern warning: "But if you don't do this, you will certainly sin against the Lord; *be sure your sin will catch up with you*" (Numbers 32:23, CSB, emphasis mine). (The NLT states, *"Your sin will find you out."*)

The reality is that God will not let any sin go by without its due punishment. He can't. He is God. He has the means and the ways to enforce his will. The seven capital sins are inescapable in our society. We think we can hide our sins but in due time, they will catch up with us and with our families. In the book of Joshua, chapter 7, we see the sad example of Achan. His greed prompted him to take some forbidden loot from Jericho and he hid his sin. However, his sin caught up with him and destroyed his family as well. We need to be aware of the reality of capital sin in our lives and its impact in our families. This is one of our major omissions. We commit the sin and think it will not impact our families. We must remember that certain characteristics of capital sin will beset us.

First, the reality of capital sin is all around us. The seven sins are our daily bread. They are everywhere and ready to pounce on our families and each of us. These sins are inescapable. Ever since the sixth century, the church has identified these sins as mainstays of destruction of our society and our families. These sins are pride, anger, sloth, lust, avarice, gluttony, and envy. You already know them by name. You know them by the path of destruction they create. You know them by the indictment of capital offenses they bring your family.

In the United States, capital offenses are those crimes that demand the death penalty as just retribution. These are the most heinous and depraved of offenses, usually involving first-degree murder and additional violations. These seven sins are the spiritual equivalent of societal capital offenses, and they are a constant part of our moral landscape. However, in our society, they are not only tolerated but accepted. These sins have become a normal part of our lives. They are all around us.

We are bound to sin. Our human nature is a sinful nature. These sins will sink you and also your family. Just as Moses warned the clans of Reuben and Gad, God is warning us today. Your sin will catch up with you and this sin will destroy your family.

ESCAPING CAPITAL PUNISHMENT

Second, the penalty of capital sin is guaranteed. The justice of God demands payment and retribution. Human justice also demands retribution for capital offenses. Since 1977, in the US, 1,540 individuals have paid with their lives for a capital offense at the hands of the US government. In the year 2020, the records show that 2,500 people were waiting for execution for a capital offense. The penalty for all capital offenses or crimes is death. Death by injection, electrocution, hanging, or firing squad is in the legal code of the United States.

The penalty for these seven capital sins is death. In fact, the penalty of sin, all sin, is death. "For all have sinned, and come short of the glory of God" (Romans 3:23, KJV). "For the wages of sin is death" (Romans 6:23, KJV). These and many other verses in the Bible testify that God does not tolerate sin. The horrible effects of sin on your family are guaranteed. Just as the death penalty is guaranteed for anyone who commits a capital offence in our country, so these capital sins spell a serious punishment for those who commit them and their families. Now here we find an unexpected surprise!

Third, every capital sin can be pardoned. There are occasions (though extremely rare) when our society pardons capital sins. The United States has a whole codified process to enable someone to appeal for *clemency*. This is not an easy process and few succeed, but the path is clearly marked.

The Bible tells us God pardons capital sins as well. Clemency is defined in the Bible as *forgiveness*. We see the explanation of forgiveness in Isaiah 1:18–20:

> "Come, let's settle this,"
> says the Lord.
> "Though your sins are scarlet,
> they will be as white as snow;
> though they are crimson red,
> they will be like wool.
> If you are willing and obedient,
> you will eat the good things of the land.
> But if you refuse and rebel,
> you will be devoured by the sword."
> For the mouth of the Lord has spoken. (CSB)

How can a person achieve God's forgiveness? Well, technically no one can plea clemency and obtain forgiveness from God. The truth is that only God can make that case on our behalf. This is the reason Jesus died on the cross for us and was resurrected from the dead on the third day. Jesus paid the penalty of sin with his body and his blood and conquered the punishment of sin, which was death, by his resurrection. Both the death of Jesus on the cross outside Jerusalem and his subsequent resurrection from the dead are specific historical facts that underlie the Gospel/Good News and are the specific parts of God's plan that provide clemency for our sin.

Your family depends on you to make a positive difference on their behalf. You do this by deciding to trust and believe God. This is a decision you make now, this instant, but it will affect your family for generations. Yes, this choice means that you and your family will survive the seven sins that can sink your family!

REFLECTION QUESTIONS

1. Would you agree that you could stop the effects of cross-generational sin if you wanted to stop it?

2. Do you believe that the seven capital sins are ubiquitous in our society?

3. How do these sins affect you? Do you have a favorite sin you commit over and over?

4. Would you like to stop it all now? Would you like to be the person in your family that puts a stop to cross-generational sin?

PRAYER

The Lord's Prayer (Matthew 6:9–13, CSB)
"Our Father in heaven,
your name be honored as holy.
Your kingdom come.
Your will be done
on earth as it is in heaven.
Give us today our daily bread.
And forgive us our debts,
as we also have forgiven our debtors.
And do not bring us into temptation,
but deliver us from the evil one.
For yours is the kingdom, and the power, and the glory forever.
Amen."

Author's Note

Dear Reader,

Thank you for finishing this book. It is my desire as an author that the lessons I have learned I can share with you. I hope the words in this book make a difference in your life as they have in mine. I wish you well in your efforts to right your family's ship.

Please, if you can and so desire, go to my web page www.davidlemajr.org and share your testimony of how God helped you navigate these waters. Also, there you will find information about our ministry and other books and resources that may interest you.

Thank you!

ABOUT THE AUTHOR

About The Author

The author, Dr. Lema, is highly qualified to speak on this subject. He has a PhD in Pastoral Ministry (Missions) and a DMin in Leadership from NOBTS. He has years of experience as a professor, pastor, husband, and father who has walked a long road in life experience.

More About Maven House Publishing

Maven House Publishing is an extension of the Maven House Movement, with the purpose of bringing stories inspired by The Holy Spirit to life. Maven in Hebrew means "He who understands." Maven House is a community of women seeking to grow in their understanding of God and the world and, as part of that growth, share their stories.

Our vision is to bring to the world the story that God has given you from your heart. We partner with beginning and returning authors to complete, edit, publish, and print their written masterpiece. If you are ready to share the story God has placed in you, contact our team today!

The Maven House Movement

Maven House, was founded by Vanessa Gracia Cruz in 2021, as a community of multi-passionate women, with a passion to reach their full potential in Christ. A Maven is an expert with knowledge and experience in an area, which has been obtained informally. At Maven House, we believe in putting the tools directly in the hands of the woman who wants to spearhead her own personal development and leadership. The Maven House movement is about inspiring women to discover their true identity and learn to use their God-given talents to build the Kingdom of God. The Maven House platform offers courses, Bible studies, resources, monthly support, and a community of women. Through membership in this community, they can seek advice, develop ideas, attend events and enjoy access to a wide network of contacts; all with the vision of empowering and connect women of God.

MAVEN HOUSE PUBLISHING

Do you want to join the community?
Scan this code to join Maven House today
Becomeamaven.com | mavenhousepublishing.com

APPENDIX

Appendix A

How God Atoned for Your Sins and Your Family's Sins

The Three Circles

Please go to the following website for specific information on the Three Circles: https://vimeo.com/227782208.

Endnotes

1 Wikipedia, s.v. "pride," Wikipedia.org, updated July 12, 2024, https://en.wikipedia.org/wiki/Pride.
2 John Maxwell, "The Problem of Pride," johnmaxwell.com, John C. Maxwell, January 22, 2014, https://www.johnmaxwell.com/blog/the-problem-of-pride/.
3 Wikipedia, s.v. "pride."
4 "The Bible & Pride," Risen Church, May 17, 2022, Facebook post, https://www.facebook.com/Risen473/photos/a.650021058743828/1384351368644123/?type=3&_rdr.
5 Oxford English Dictionary Online, s.v. "pride," accessed April 13, 2024, https://www.oed.com/dictionary/pride_n1?tab=meaning_and_use#28314327.
6 Dictionary.com, s.v. "pride," Dictionary.com, accessed April 13, 2024, https://www.dictionary.com/browse/pride.
7 "The Deliverer Delivered (by Women)!" LigonDuncan.com, October 8, 2000, https://ligonduncan.com/the-deliverer-delivered-by-women-1071/.
8 Rick Warren, The Purpose Driven Life (Grand Rapids, MI: Zondervan, 2002), 265.
9 Wikipedia, s.v. "Anger," Wikipedia.org, updated July 18, 2024, https://en.wikipedia.org/wiki/Anger.
10 "Anger," American Psychological Association website, Psychology Topics, accessed August 10, 2024, https://www.apa.org/topics/anger.
11 James E. Smith, The College Press NIV Commentary: 1 and 2 Samuel (Joplin, MO: College Press Publishing Company, Inc., 2024), section 13:11–14.
12 Smith, 1 and 2 Samuel, section 13:11–14.
13 Craig E. Morrison, Berit Olam, Studies in Hebrew Narrative &

Poetry: 1 and 2 Samuel (Collegeville, MN: Liturgical Press, 2013), see commentary on 13:7 and note 62.

14   Commentary on 2 Samuel 13:21, CBS, bible.com, accessed August 10, 2024, https://www.bible.com/bible/1713/2SA.13.CSB.

15   Rae Jacobson, "Teens and Anger," childmind.org, Child Mind Institute, updated May 21, 2024, https://childmind.org/article/teens-and-anger/.

16   Jacobson, "Teens and Anger."

17   Jacobson, "Teens and Anger."

18   Jacobson, "Teens and Anger."

19   Jacobson, "Teens and Anger."

20   Robert D. Bergen, 1, 2 Samuel: The New American Commentary: An Exegetical and Theological Exposition of Holy Scripture, vol. 7 (Nashville, Holman Reference, 1996), see commentary on 2 Samuel 13.

21   John Ortberg, "Confessions of a Lazy Pastor," in Richard Exley, Makr Galli, and John Ortberg, Dangers, Toils & Snares: Resisting the Hidden Temptations of Ministry, Mastering Ministry's Pressure Points (Sisters, OR: Multnomah Books, 1994), 51.

22   "Sloth," WWF, Species, worldwildlife.org, accessed August 10, 2024, https://www.worldwildlife.org/species/sloth#:~:text=Sloths%E2%80%94the%20sluggish%20tree%2Ddwellers,20%20hours%20per%20day%20sleeping.

23   Paul Lee Tan, Encyclopedia of 7700 Illustrations: Signs of the Times (Garland, TX: Bible Communications, Inc., 1996, electronic edition), 1301.

24   Wikipedia, s.v. "acedia," Wikipedia.org, updated June 24, 2024, https://en.wikipedia.org/wiki/Acedia

25   Wikipedia, s.v. "acedia."

26   Archibald Browning Drysdale Alexander, "Seven Deadly Sins," Encyclopedia of Religion and Ethics, ed. James Hastings, John A. Selbie, and Louis H. Gray (Edinburgh; New York: T. & T. Clark; Charles Scribner's Sons, 1908–26), 427–28.

27   John Cassian, "The Twelve Books of John Cassian on the Institutes of the Cœnobia," in Sulpitius Severus, Vincent of Lérins, John Cassian, ed. Philip Schaff and Henry Wace, trans. Edgar C. S. Gibson, vol. 11, A Select Library of the Nicene and Post-Nicene Fathers of the Christian Church, Second Series (New York: Christian Literature Company, 1894), 233–34.

28   Cassian, The Twelve Books, 266.
29   Wikipedia, s.v. "acedia."
30   "Acedia = Lack of Care," Path to the Maypole of Wisdom: A Case for Spiritual Ethics, Virtues, and Uprightness in Our Times, accessed August 18, 2024, https://maypoleofwisdom.com/acedia-lack-of-care-disease-of-our-times/.
31   Wikipedia, s.v. "Seven Deadly Sins," Wikipedia.org, updated August 10, 2024, https://en.wikipedia.org/wiki/Seven_deadly_sins. See also Stanford M. Lyman, The Seven Deadly Sins: Society and Evil, expanded ed. (Lanham, MD: Rowman & Littlefield Publisher, 1989), 6–7.
32   Wikipedia, s.v. "Seven Deadly Sins."
33   Kathleen Norris, Acedia and Me: A Marriage, Monks, and a Writer's Life (New York: Riverhead Books, 2008).
34   William Hendriksen, <u>Comentario Al Nuevo Testamento: El Evangelio Según San Mateo</u> (Grand Rapids, MI: Libros Desafío, 2007), 889.
35   Mary Fairchild, "How Heavy Was a Talent in the Bible?" Learn Religions, Christianity, updated on July 19, 2024, https://www.learnreligions.com/what-is-a-talent-700699.
36   John Peter Lange and Philip Schaff, <u>A Commentary on the Holy Scriptures: Matthew</u> (Bellingham, WA: Logos Bible Software, 2008), 444.
37   "Hakuna Matata," The Lion King, Disney, lyrics by Tim Rice, music by Elton John.
38   See Matthew 5:28, CSB. Other versions read differently. Some, like the KJV, translate lust as a noun, e.g. "anyone who looks at a woman with lust . . ."
39   Michael P. Green, ed., <u>Illustrations for Biblical Preaching: Over 1500 Sermon Illustrations Arranged by Topic and Indexed Exhaustively</u>, rev. ed. of The Expositor's Illustration File (Grand Rapids, MI: Baker Book House, 1989).
40   Vocabulary.com, s.v. "lust," accessed November 08, 2023, https://www.vocabulary.com/dictionary/lust.
41   Read the story in 2 Samuel 11:5–25.
42   Smith, 1 and 2 Samuel, 428.
43   E. J. Mundell, "Lust Strikes Both Genders Daily," HealthDay.com, Sexual Health, May 28, 2005, https://www.healthday.com/health-news/sexual-health/lust-strikes-both-genders-daily-525971.html .

44   Mundell, "Lust Strikes Both Genders Daily."
45   Statistics provided by the World Obesity Atlas 2023, World Obesity Federation, https://s3-eu-west-1.amazonaws.com/wof-files/World_Obesity_Atlas_2023_Report.pdf, 10, accessed August 10, 2023.
46   Linda Searing, "51 Percent of World Population May Be Overweight or Obese by 2035," The Washington Post, washingtonpost.com, Wellness, May 20, 2023, https://www.washingtonpost.com/wellness/2023/03/20/obesity-overweight-increasing-worldwide/.
47   Rick Warren, Daniel Amen, and Mark Hyman, The Daniel Plan (Grand Rapids, MI: Zondervan, 2013), 13.
48   "Childhood Obesity," Our World in Data, Obesity, ourworldindata.org, accessed August 10, 2024, https://ourworldindata.org/obesity#childhood-obesity.
49   "Explore Data by Demographic, Ages 10–17," State of Childhood Obesity, Robert Wood Johnson Foundation, stateofchildhoodobesity.org, accessed August 10, 2024, https://stateofchildhoodobesity.org/demographic-data/ages-10-17/#:~:text=Roughly%20one%20in%20six%20youth,10%20to%2017%20had%20obesity.
50   Emily Laurence, "Obesity Statistics and Facts in 2024," Forbes Health, updated January 10, 2024, https://www.forbes.com/health/body/obesity-statistics/#:~:text=Worldwide%2C%20more%20than%201%20billion,million%20children%2C%20according%20to%20WHO.
51   Wikipedia, s.v. "Seven Deadly Sins."
52   Brittannica Online, s.v. "gluttony," accessed August 10, 2024, https://www.britannica.com/topic/gluttony.
53   Brittanica, s.v. "gluttony."
54   "Bible Verses About Gluttony," Bible Study Tools, compiled February 16, 2024, biblestudytools.com, https://www.biblestudytools.com/topical-verses/bible-verses-about-gluttony/.
55   Mary Fairchild, "What Does the Bible Say About Gluttony?" Learn Religions, updated June 29, 2019, learnreligions.com, Christianity, https://www.learnreligions.com/gluttony-in-the-bible-4689201#:~:text=%E2%80%9CThe%20Son%20of%20Man%20came,average%20person%20in%20his%20day.
56   Kim Montgomery, "What Is Gluttony?" Ligonier, April 17, 2023, ligonier.org, Life Issues, https://www.ligonier.org/learn/articles/virtues-vices-gluttony#:~:text=Gluttony%2C%20biblically%20speak-

ing%2C%20can%20be,soul%20(the%20inner%20person).
57 Fairchild, "What Does the Bible Say About Gluttony?"
58 Lisa Kutolowski, "The Spirit of Gluttony or How Noticing Our Thoughts Invites Freedom." Metanoia of Vermont, February 9, 2021, metanoiavt.com, https://www.metanoiavt.com/reflections/2021/2/9/freedom-from-unthinking-thoughts-about-food.
59 Jason Liske, "The Seven Deadly Sins: Gluttony," The Catholic Gentleman, November 5, 2013, catholicgentleman.com, https://catholicgentleman.com/2013/11/the-seven-deadly-sins-gluttony/.
60 Yourdictionary.com, s.v. "greed," accessed August 10, 2024, https://www.yourdictionary.com/greed.
61 Vocabulary.com, s.v. "greed," accessed August 10, 2024, https://www.vocabulary.com/dictionary/greed.
62 Loose translation by the author of Luke 12:16–20.
63 Leo Tolstoy, How Much Land Does a Man Need? (Online: The Floating Press, 2016).
64 Tolstoy, How Much Land Does a Man Need?
65 Merriam-Webster, s.v. "envy," accessed August 10, 2024, https://www.merriam-webster.com/dictionary/envy.
66 From Ralph Waldo Emerson's essay on Self Reliance, Owl Eyes, Library, Nonfiction, Self-Reliance, owleyes.org, accessed August 18, 2024, cf p. 1, https://www.owleyes.org/text/self-reliance.

Made in the USA
Columbia, SC
24 October 2024